Copyright ©2023 by Meredith Avren

Written by Meredith Avren, M.Ed., CCC-SLP
Illustrated by Josh Avren

All rights reserved. No part of this book, may be reproduced, transmitted, or stored in an information retrieval system in any form or by any means, graphic, electronic, or mechanical, including photocopying, taping and recording, without prior written permission from the publisher. In accordance of the U.S. Copyright Act of 1976, any violation is unlawful piracy and theft of the author's and illustrator's intellectual property.

If you would like to use material from this book other than for personal use, prior written premission must be obtained by contacting the publisher at permissions@avrenbooks.com. Thank you for your support of the creators' rights.

R Sound Chaining - First Edition 2023

Library of Congress Catalog Card Number Pending

ISBN 978-0-9995964-6-3
10 9 8 7 6 5 4 3 2 1

Published by Avren Books™

PEACHIE SPEECHIE'S
R SOUND CHAINING

Contents

What Is Chaining? Introduction	5-6
How To Say The R Sound	7
R Sound Practice	8
R Sound Chaining Data Sheet	9
R Sound Chaining Video Page	10
Self Rating Cards	11
/ɹi/ ree	13-36
/ɹɪ/ rih	37-48
/ɹe/ ray	49-72
/ɹo/ row	73-84
/ɹɑ/ rah	85-98
/ɹɛ/ reh	99-112
/ɹæ/ ra	113-134
/ɹu/ roo	135-146
/ɹʌ/ ruh	147-160
/ɹaɪ/ rye	161-168
/dɹ/	169-186
/tɹ/	187-200
/ʃɹ/ shr	201-208
ER	209-228
AR	229-260
EAR	261-282
IRE	283-298
AIR	299-342
OR	343-368
L→R	369-376
Blank Chaining Template	377
Resources	379
About the Author	381

Mouths and other visuals may not be transmitted, copied, duplicated or reproduced in whole or part by any means.

R Sound Chaining
by Peachie Speechie

About this workbook

Thank you for purchasing R Sound Chaining. This workbook is designed for speech-language pathologists to use during therapy sessions with their students/clients. It includes visuals and words for teaching the R sound using chaining. I created it to provide clear, helpful, visuals that engage children during the therapy session. I hope you love it! If you have any questions, please reach out to me at meredith@peachiespeechie.com

What is speech chaining?

Chaining is a treatment approach during which you build on pre-trained sounds, gradually increasing the complexity of speech movements. For example, your student would say ray → raise → raisin → raisin cookie. The targets in this example are "chained", building on the base utterance, "ray". The complexity of the speech movements and length of utterance increases as you move through the chain.

Chaining is a popular technique, particularly for children with apraxia of speech or more severe speech sound disorders. You'll often hear SLPs talk about forward chaining and backward chaining. Forward chaining is when you start with the beginning of an utterance and work forward. For example, focusing on "ma" and then adding the "me" to get to "mommy". Backward chaining is when you start at the end and work backward to the start of the word. For example, focusing on "pen" and then adding "oh" to get "open".

Speech motor chaining takes the principles of motor learning into consideration and has resulted in successful acquisition of target speech patterns and generalization to untrained words (Preston, Leece & Storto, 2019). You can use chaining to help students advance from the syllable level production of the R sound to production in sentences.

Want to learn about speech motor chaining in more detail? Check out this article: Tutorial: Speech Motor Chaining Treatment for School-Age Children With Speech Sound Disorders.

How do I use these worksheets in my sessions?

First, you'll want to elicit the R sound using the elicitation page. Provide your student with specific placement instructions and visuals to help them achieve accurate production. Once you've established stimulabilty for the R sound, you're ready to move on to the chaining worksheets. You'll start at the syllable level, and then move to monosyllabic words, multisyllabic words, phrases, and then sentences. In their tutorial article, Preston, Leece, and Storto (2019) suggest having students practice self-generated sentences. You can have your students do this instead of using the sentences provided if desired.

Start with the syllable level target, and practice it multiple times. If they get it correct 5-6 times, move on to the next level in the chain. If they have difficulty and can't produce an accurate R in the next level, move back a level and practice there. This means you may be practicing at the syllable, word, and sentence level all within one session! Aim for a high number of trials, and be sure to give your student feedback.

Your student can use the How did my R Sound? self-rating scales to indicate whether they thought they had an accurate or inaccurate production. You can cut these out of the workbook, or make photocopies for your students to use.

Enjoy these chaining worksheets in your R sound therapy sessions! Don't forget to check out my other materials, including Coarticulation for the R Sound and I Can Say the R Sound. You can scan these QR codes to access these additional workbooks and Peachie Speechie's free video library.

Meredith Avren, M.Ed., CCC-SLP

Peachie Speechie Videos

Coarticulation for the R Sound

I Can Say the R Sound

Mouths and other visuals may not be transmitted, copied, duplicated or reproduced in whole or part by any means.

How To Say The R Sound

Give your student specific placement instructions and show them the visuals below to help them say the R sound. Additionally, you can watch free instructional videos for the R sound online at PeachieSpeechie.com/videos.

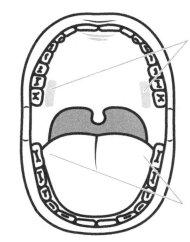

Back sides of tongue lift and touch the spot inside the back teeth

Back sides of tongue

Bunched R

To make the R sound, the back sides of your tongue lift to touch the "tongue bracing spots" inside your back teeth.

With the back sides lifted, there will be a groove in the middle. You can call this the taco tongue position.

The blade of your tongue will be lifted a bit. Your tongue will pull back and be tense. Your voice will be on.

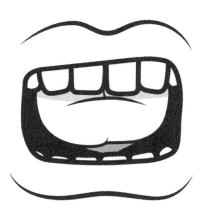

Retroflex R

Another way to make the R sound is by using the retroflex tongue position. To do this, lift the tip of your tongue up and curl it back.

The back sides of your tongue will be lifted and your voice will be on.

R Sound Practice

Look at the pictures and placement instructions on the previous page. Practice getting your tongue into position and saying the R sound. Mark a box each time you practice. There are 100 boxes total.

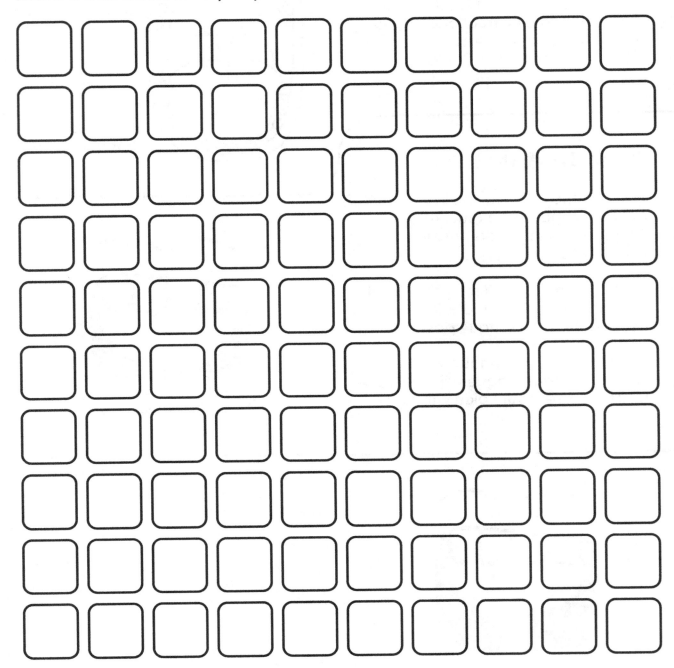

Great job practicing!

R Sound Chaining Data Sheet

Name: _____ Clinician: _____

Date:	Notes:
Syllable	
Monosyllabic word	
Multisyllabic word	
Phrase	
Sentence	

Date:	Notes:
Syllable	
Monosyllabic word	
Multisyllabic word	
Phrase	
Sentence	

Date:	Notes:
Syllable	
Monosyllabic word	
Multisyllabic word	
Phrase	
Sentence	

Date:	Notes:
Syllable	
Monosyllabic word	
Multisyllabic word	
Phrase	
Sentence	

Date:	Notes:
Syllable	
Monosyllabic word	
Multisyllabic word	
Phrase	
Sentence	

PEACHIE SPEECHIE'S
R SOUND CHAINING

VIDEO PAGE

Use this page to follow along with the video.

Start with a syllable-level utterance and grdually add to it.

VIEW THIS VIDEO AT PEACHIESPEECHIE.COM/VIDEOS

Ree
⇩
Read
⇩
Reading
⇩
Reading assignment
⇩
Did you complete your reading assignment?

Ray
⇩
Rain
⇩
Raincoat
⇩
Need a raincoat
⇩

Rye
⇩
Rhyme
⇩
Rhyming
⇩
Rhyming words
⇩

Are
⇩
Par
⇩
Parking
⇩
Parking spot
⇩

WRITE YOUR OWN SENTENCE USING THE PHRASE ABOVE

PEACHIE SPEECHIE'S
R SOUND CHAINING
SELF RATING

Cut out the cards below. Select which one you'd like to use. After your student produces the R sound, ask them to rate their own production. Let them know if you agree or disagree with their rating.

R SOUND CHAINING

/ɹi/

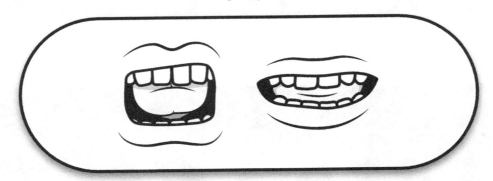

Ree
⇩
Read
⇩
Reading
⇩
Reading assignment
⇩
Did you complete your reading assignment?

PEACHIE SPEECHIE'S
R SOUND CHAINING

/ɹi/

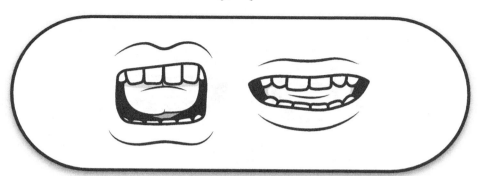

Ree
⇩
Reach
⇩
Reaching
⇩
Reaching out
⇩
Thanks for reaching out when I was sick.

PEACHIE SPEECHIE'S
R SOUND CHAINING

/ɹi/

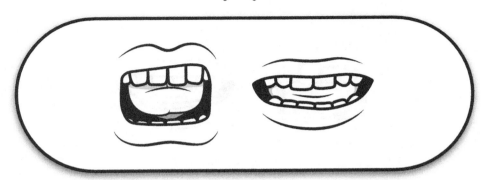

Ree
⇩
Reez
⇩
Reason
⇩
Good reason
⇩
He had a good reason for not being there.

PEACHIE SPEECHIE'S
R SOUND CHAINING

/ɹi/

Ree
⇩
Real
⇩
Reeling
⇩
Reeling in
⇩
He was reeling in his fish at the dock.

PEACHIE SPEECHIE'S
R SOUND CHAINING

/ɹi/

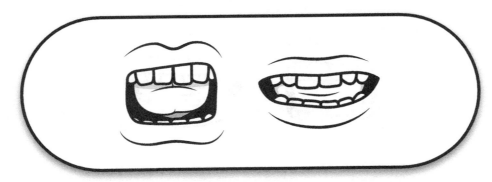

Ree
⇩
Reap
⇩
Repeat
⇩
Repeat the question
⇩
Can you please repeat the question for me?

PEACHIE SPEECHIE'S
R SOUND CHAINING

/ɹi/

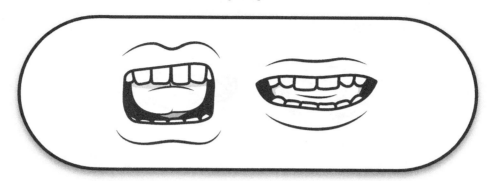

Ree

⇩

Reese

⇩

Respectful

⇩

Should be respectful

⇩

You should be respectful to your teachers.

PEACHIE SPEECHIE'S
R SOUND CHAINING

/ɹi/

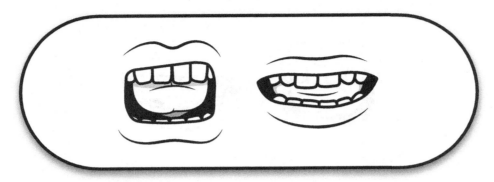

Ree

⇩

Reem

⇩

Remember

⇩

Can't remember

⇩

I can't remember the building address.

PEACHIE SPEECHIE'S
R SOUND CHAINING

/ɹi/

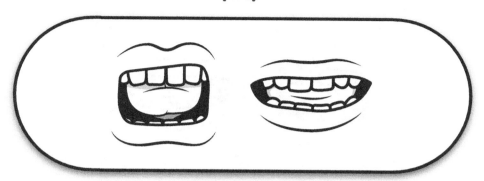

Ree
⇩
Reak
⇩
Recall
⇩
Do you recall
⇩
Do you recall the name of that book?

PEACHIE SPEECHIE'S
R SOUND CHAINING

/ɹi/

Ree
⇩
Reep
⇩
Report
⇩
Report card
⇩
Please show me your report card.

PEACHIE SPEECHIE'S
R SOUND CHAINING

/ɹi/

Ree
⇩
Reef
⇩
Refill
⇩
Another refill
⇩
Do you need another refill?

PEACHIE SPEECHIE'S
R SOUND CHAINING

/ɹi/

Ree
⇩
Reed
⇩
Redo
⇩
Redo it all
⇩
I messed up, so I have to redo it all.

PEACHIE SPEECHIE'S
R SOUND CHAINING

/ɹi/

Ree
⇩
Reece
⇩
Recess
⇩
Time for recess
⇩
Is it time for recess yet?

Peachie Speechie's
R SOUND CHAINING

/ɹi/

Ree
⇩
Reem
⇩
Remove
⇩
Remove it
⇩
Please remove it from the list.

PEACHIE SPEECHIE'S
R SOUND CHAINING

/ɹi/

Ree

⇩

Reep

⇩

Replace

⇩

Replace the sofa

⇩

We had to replace the sofa with a new one.

PEACHIE SPEECHIE'S
R SOUND CHAINING

/ɹi/

Ree
⇩
Reef
⇩
Refund
⇩
Need a refund
⇩
I need a refund on that purchase.

Peachie Speechie's
R Sound Chaining

/ɹi/

Ree

Reek

Recline

Want to recline

⇩

I want to recline in my comfy chair.

PEACHIE SPEECHIE'S
R SOUND CHAINING

/ɹi/

Ree
⇩
Reep
⇩
Reply
⇩
Did you reply?
⇩
Did you reply to the message?

PEACHIE SPEECHIE'S
R SOUND CHAINING

/ɹi/

Ree

⇩

Reem

⇩

Remote

⇩

Find the remote

⇩

I can't find the remote.

PEACHIE SPEECHIE'S
R SOUND CHAINING

/ɹi/

Ree
⇩
Reek
⇩
Request
⇩
Request a change
⇩
I need to request a change in my schedule.

PEACHIE SPEECHIE'S
R SOUND CHAINING

/ɹi/

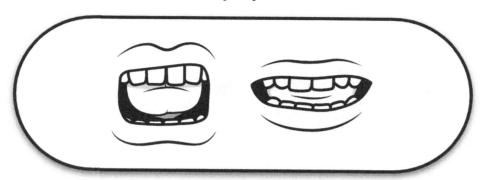

Ree
⇩
Reej
⇩
Reject
⇩
Reject the offer
⇩
I had to reject the offer.

PEACHIE SPEECHIE'S
R SOUND CHAINING

/ɹi/

Ree
⇩
Read
⇩
Redeem
⇩
Redeem the coupon
⇩
I can redeem the coupon at the shop.

PEACHIE SPEECHIE'S
R SOUND CHAINING

/ɹi/

Ree

⇩

Tree

⇩

Treetops

⇩

See the treetops

⇩

I can see the treetops from my window.

PEACHIE SPEECHIE'S
R SOUND CHAINING

/ɹɪ/

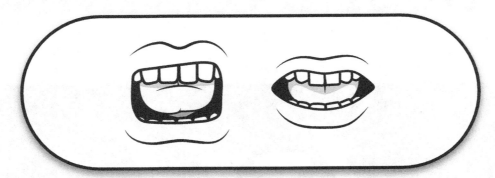

Rih
⇩
Rip
⇩
Ripping
⇩
I'm ripping it
⇩
I made a mistake on this paper, so I'm ripping it up.

Peachie Speechie's
R Sound Chaining

/ɹɪ/

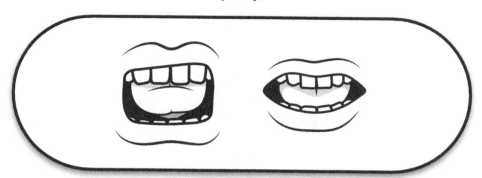

Rih

⇩

Rich

⇩

Riches

⇩

All the riches

⇩

With all the riches in the world, you still can't buy happiness.

PEACHIE SPEECHIE'S
R SOUND CHAINING

/ɹɪ/

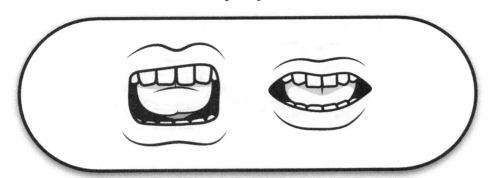

Rih
⇩
Rib
⇩
Ribbon
⇩
Long pink ribbon
⇩
She wore a long pink ribbon in her hair.

PEACHIE SPEECHIE'S
R SOUND CHAINING

/ɹɪ/

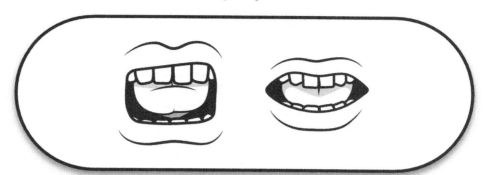

Rih
⇩
Ring
⇩
Ringing
⇩
The phone ringing
⇩
Do you hear the phone ringing upstairs?

PEACHIE SPEECHIE'S
R SOUND CHAINING

/ɪr/

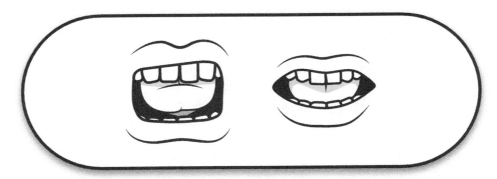

Rih

Risk

Risky

Risky business

Lending money to people you don't know is a risky business.

PEACHIE SPEECHIE'S
R SOUND CHAINING

/ɪr/

Rih
⇩
Rid
⇩
Ridden
⇩
Ridden a bike
⇩
Have you ever ridden a bike before?

PEACHIE SPEECHIE'S
R SOUND CHAINING

/ɹɪ/

Rih
⇩
Rid
⇩
Ridicule
⇩
Ridicule people
⇩
It's not nice to ridicule people.

PEACHIE SPEECHIE'S
R SOUND CHAINING

/ɪr/

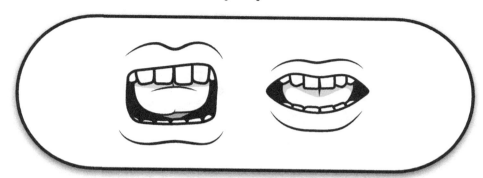

Rih
⇩
Rick
⇩
Ricky
⇩
You know Ricky
⇩
Do you know Ricky, the baseball coach?

PEACHIE SPEECHIE'S
R SOUND CHAINING

/ɹɪ/

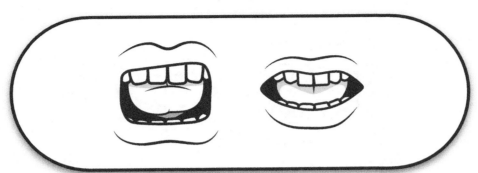

Rih
⇩
Rin
⇩
Siren
⇩
Loud siren
⇩
Listen to the loud siren.

PEACHIE SPEECHIE'S
R SOUND CHAINING

/ɹɪ/

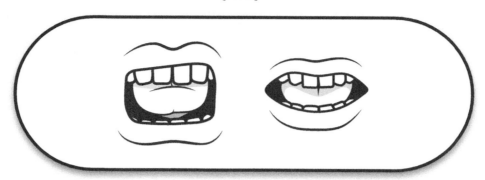

Rih
⇩
Rin
⇩
Karen
⇩
Call me Karen
⇩
Hello, you can call me Karen.

PEACHIE SPEECHIE'S
R SOUND CHAINING

/ɹe/

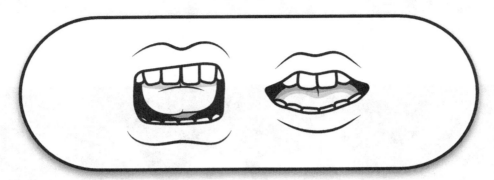

Ray
⇩
Rain
⇩
Rainbow
⇩
Big rainbow
⇩
I saw a big rainbow in the sky.

PEACHIE SPEECHIE'S
R SOUND CHAINING

/ɹe/

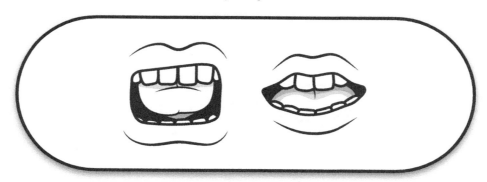

Ray
⇩
Race
⇩
Racing
⇩
Racing game
⇩
We are playing a racing game on the playground.

PEACHIE SPEECHIE'S
R SOUND CHAINING

/ɹe/

Ray
⇩
Rave
⇩
Raven
⇩
Black raven
⇩
The black raven is flying in the sky.

Peachie Speechie's
R Sound Chaining

/ɹe/

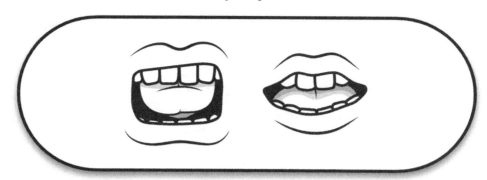

Ray
⇩
Rail
⇩
Railway
⇩
Railway station
⇩
She is waiting at the railway station.

PEACHIE SPEECHIE'S
R SOUND CHAINING

/ɹe/

Ray
⇩
Rake
⇩
Raking
⇩
Raking leaves
⇩
We are raking leaves outside.

R SOUND CHAINING

/ɹe/

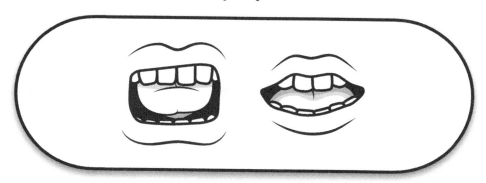

Ray
⇩
Raise
⇩
Raisin
⇩
Raisin cookies
⇩
Mom is baking raisin cookies.

PEACHIE SPEECHIE'S
R SOUND CHAINING

/ɹe/

Ray

⇩

Rach

⇩

Rachel

⇩

Rachel Smith

⇩

Rachel Smith is a girl at my school.

PEACHIE SPEECHIE'S
R SOUND CHAINING

/ɹe/

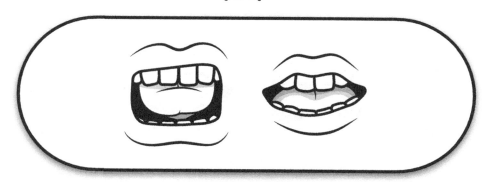

Ray

⇩

Raid

⇩

Raided

⇩

Raided the fridge

⇩

I raided the fridge last night.

PEACHIE SPEECHIE'S
R SOUND CHAINING

/ɹe/

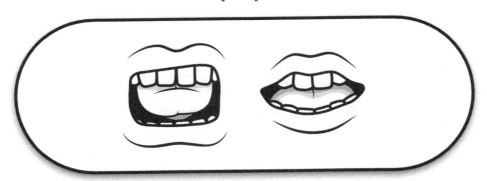

Ray
⇩
Rain
⇩
Raincoat
⇩
Need a raincoat
⇩
You'll need a raincoat today.

PEACHIE SPEECHIE'S
R SOUND CHAINING

/ɹe/

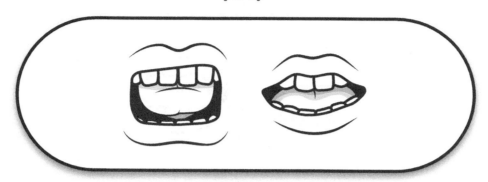

Ray
⇩
Rate
⇩
Rating
⇩
What's the rating?
⇩
What's the rating on that movie?

PEACHIE SPEECHIE'S
R SOUND CHAINING

/ɹe/

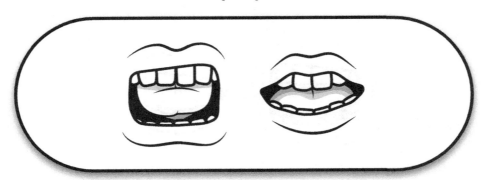

Ray

Rave

Raving

Raving about

She was raving about the delicious cake.

PEACHIE SPEECHIE'S
R SOUND CHAINING

/ɹe/

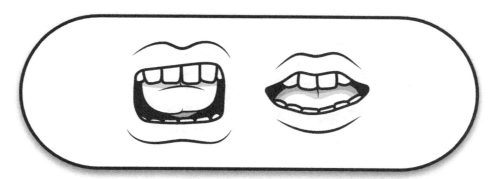

Ray
⇩
Raid
⇩
Radio
⇩
Radio station
⇩
What is your favorite radio station?

PEACHIE SPEECHIE'S
R SOUND CHAINING

/ɹe/

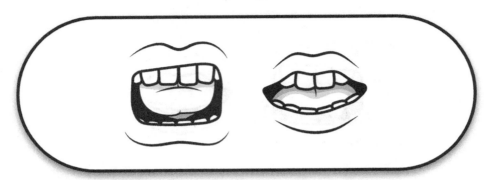

Ray
⇩
Raid
⇩
Radiant
⇩
Looked radiant
⇩
Mom looked radiant in that dress.

Peachie Speechie's
R Sound Chaining

/ɹe/

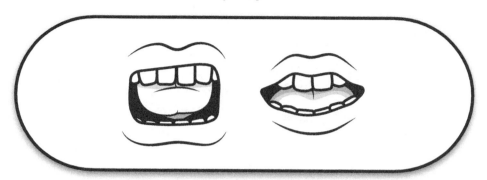

Ray
⇩
Raid
⇩
Radar
⇩
Detected by radar
⇩
The planes were detected by radar.

PEACHIE SPEECHIE'S
R SOUND CHAINING

/ɹe/

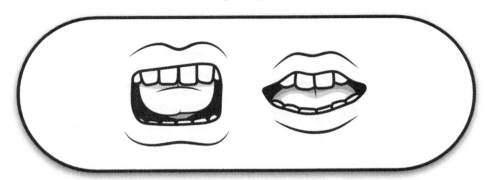

Ray
⇩
Rain
⇩
Rainy
⇩
Rainy day
⇩
It was a cold and rainy day.

PEACHIE SPEECHIE'S
R SOUND CHAINING

/ɹe/

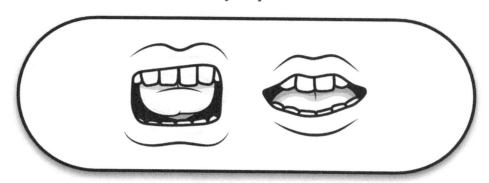

Ray
⇩
Spray
⇩
Spraying
⇩
Spraying water
⇩
He is spraying water on the plants.

PEACHIE SPEECHIE'S
R SOUND CHAINING

/ɹe/

Ray

⇩

Rays

⇩

Stingrays

⇩

Saw stingrays

⇩

I saw stingrays in the ocean.

PEACHIE SPEECHIE'S
R SOUND CHAINING

/ɹe/

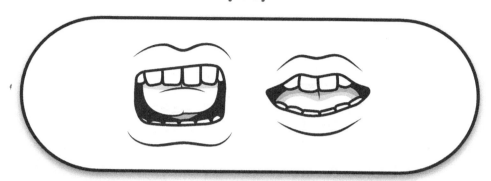

Ray
⇩
Cray
⇩
Crayon
⇩
Blue crayon
⇩
Will you please hand me the blue crayon?

PEACHIE SPEECHIE'S
R SOUND CHAINING

/ɹe/

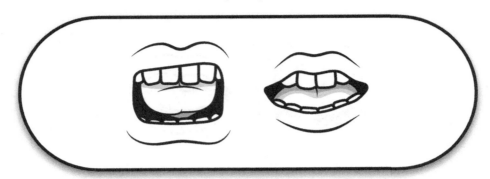

Ray
⇩
Grey
⇩
Greyhounds
⇩
Fast greyhounds
⇩
Did you know how fast greyhounds are?

Peachie Speechie's
R SOUND CHAINING

/ɹe/

Ray
⇩
Tray
⇩
Betrayed
⇩
Felt betrayed
⇩
She felt betrayed by her friend.

PEACHIE SPEECHIE'S
R SOUND CHAINING

/ɹe/

Ray
⇩
Rate
⇩
Irate
⇩
Was irate
⇩
My mother was irate when I stayed out past my curfew.

Peachie Speechie's
R Sound Chaining

/ɹe/

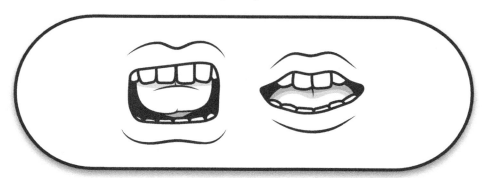

Ray
⇩
Rage
⇩
Outraged
⇩
Felt outraged
⇩
The people felt outraged.

PEACHIE SPEECHIE'S
R SOUND CHAINING

/ɹo/

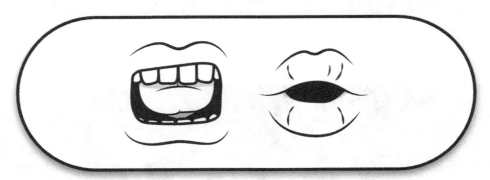

Row
⇩
Rose
⇩
Roses
⇩
Yellow roses
⇩
My favorite flowers are yellow roses.

Peachie Speechie's
R SOUND CHAINING

/ɹo/

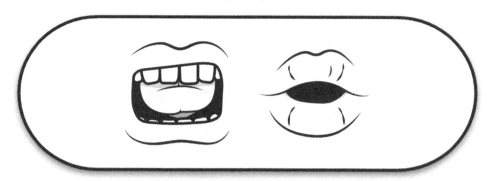

Row
⇩
Road
⇩
Roading
⇩
Off-roading
⇩
They went off-roading in the jeep.

PEACHIE SPEECHIE'S
R SOUND CHAINING

/ɹo/

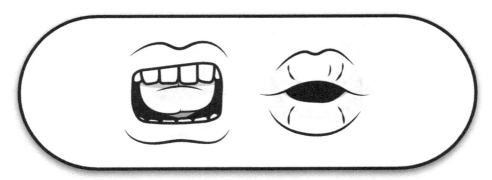

Row
⇩
Road
⇩
Rodent
⇩
Small rodent
⇩
A gerbil is a small rodent.

PEACHIE SPEECHIE'S
R SOUND CHAINING

/ɹo/

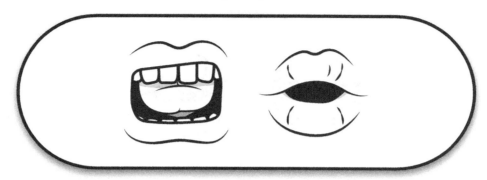

Row
⇩
Robe
⇩
Robot
⇩
New robot
⇩
Did you see the new robot at the museum?

Peachie Speechie's R SOUND CHAINING

/ɹo/

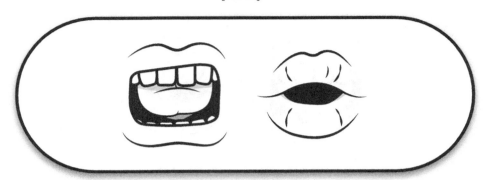

Row
⇩
Roll
⇩
Rolling
⇩
Ball is rolling
⇩
The ball is rolling down the hill.

PEACHIE SPEECHIE'S
R SOUND CHAINING

/ɹo/

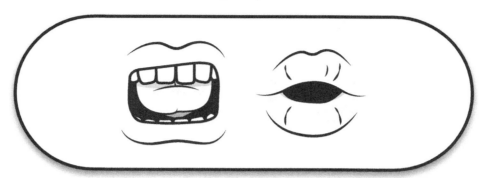

Row

⇩

Rope

⇩

Roping

⇩

Jump roping

⇩

They are jump roping on the playground.

PEACHIE SPEECHIE'S
R SOUND CHAINING

/ɹo/

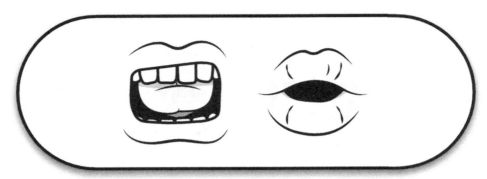

Row

⇩

Rose

⇩

Rosebuds

⇩

Saw the rosebuds

⇩

We saw the rosebuds appear on the branches.

PEACHIE SPEECHIE'S
R SOUND CHAINING

/ɹo/

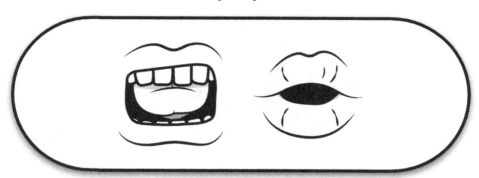

Row

⇩

Road

⇩

Rodeo

⇩

See the rodeo

⇩

Did you see the rodeo is coming to town?

PEACHIE SPEECHIE'S
R SOUND CHAINING

/ɹo/

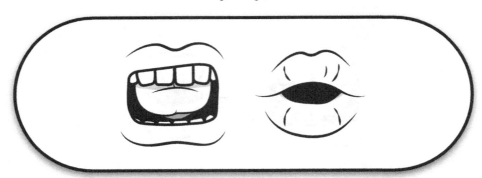

Row
⇩
Rome
⇩
Romantic
⇩
Romantic movie
⇩
We watched a romantic movie.

PEACHIE SPEECHIE'S
R SOUND CHAINING

/ɹo/

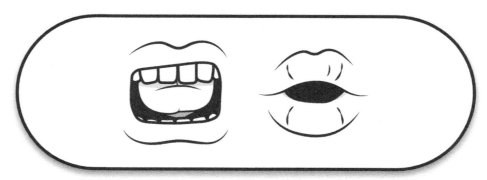

Row
⇩
Rome
⇩
Aroma
⇩
Sweet aroma
⇩
I love the sweet aroma coming from the kitchen.

PEACHIE SPEECHIE'S
R SOUND CHAINING

/ɹɑ/

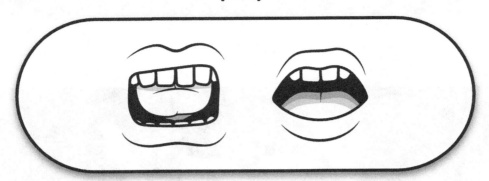

Rah
⇩
Rock
⇩
Rocking
⇩
Rocking chair
⇩
Do you want to sit in the rocking chair?

PEACHIE SPEECHIE'S
R SOUND CHAINING

/ɹɑ/

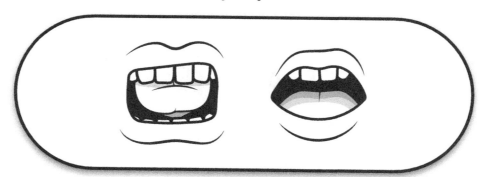

Rah
⇩
Wrong
⇩
Wrongfully
⇩
Wrongfully accused
⇩
She was wrongfully accused of taking the candy.

PEACHIE SPEECHIE'S
R SOUND CHAINING

/ɹɑ/

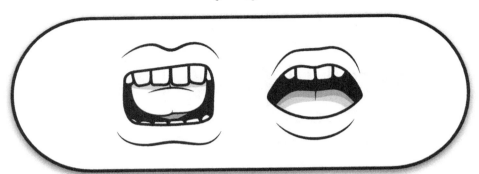

Rah
⇩
Rahm
⇩
Ramen
⇩
Ramen noodles
⇩
We made ramen noodles for lunch.

PEACHIE SPEECHIE'S
R SOUND CHAINING

/ɹa/

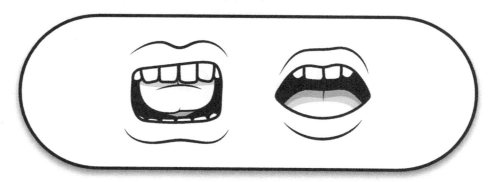

Rah
⇩
Rot
⇩
Rotting
⇩
Rotting banana
⇩
I found a rotting banana in my lunchbox.

PEACHIE SPEECHIE'S
R SOUND CHAINING

/ɹɑ/

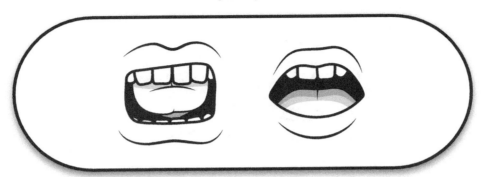

Rah
⇩
Rock
⇩
Rocket
⇩
Rocket ship
⇩
He's flying in a rocket ship.

PEACHIE SPEECHIE'S
R SOUND CHAINING

/ɹɑ/

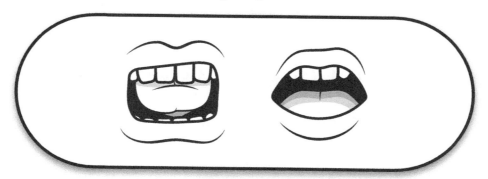

Rah

⇩

Ron

⇩

Ronald

⇩

Ronald McDonald

⇩

Ronald McDonald was a famous clown.

Peachie Speechie's
R Sound Chaining

/ɹɑ/

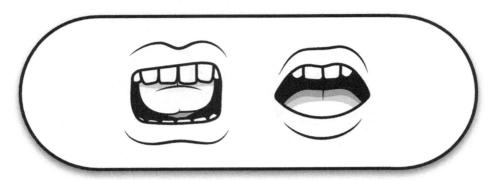

Rah
⇩
Rocks
⇩
Roxanne
⇩
Named Roxanne
⇩
My mom is named Roxanne.

PEACHIE SPEECHIE'S
R SOUND CHAINING

/ɹɑ/

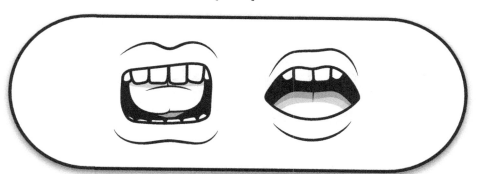

Rah
⇩
Rock
⇩
Rockies
⇩
In the Rockies
⇩
We went hiking in the Rockies.

PEACHIE SPEECHIE'S
R SOUND CHAINING

/ɹɑ/

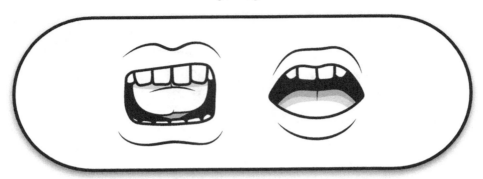

Rah
⇩
Rahm
⇩
Romping
⇩
Dogs romping
⇩
Do you see the dogs romping around the yard?

PEACHIE SPEECHIE'S
R SOUND CHAINING

/ɹɑ/

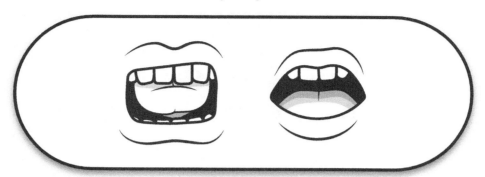

Rah
⇩
Rahl
⇩
Raleigh
⇩
City of Raleigh
⇩
Have you been to the city of Raleigh?

PEACHIE SPEECHIE'S
R SOUND CHAINING

/ɹɑ/

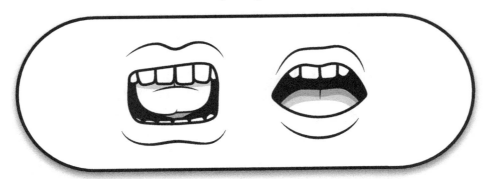

Rah
⇩
Rob
⇩
Robin
⇩
Little robin
⇩
The little robin was in the nest.

Peachie Speechie's
R Sound Chaining

/ɹɑ/

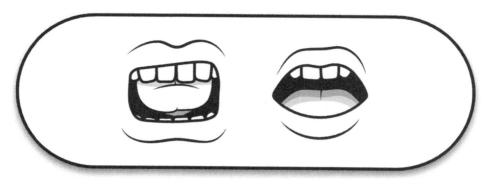

Rah
⇩
Ron
⇩
Ronda
⇩
Find Ronda
⇩
Can you help me find Ronda?

PEACHIE SPEECHIE'S
R SOUND CHAINING

/ɝ/

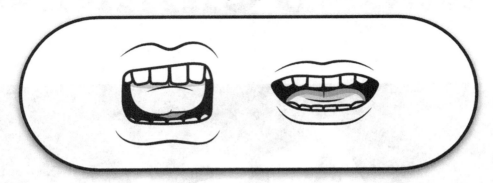

Reh
⇩
Rent
⇩
Renting
⇩
Renting a house
⇩
My aunt is renting a house nearby.

PEACHIE SPEECHIE'S
R SOUND CHAINING

/ɹɛ/

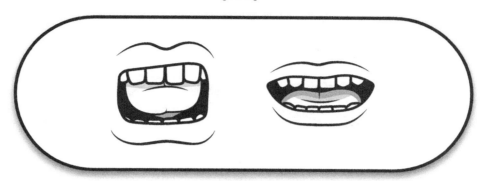

Reh
⇩
Reck
⇩
Recognize
⇩
Recognize him
⇩
Do you recognize him from the photo?

PEACHIE SPEECHIE'S
R SOUND CHAINING

/ɝ/

Reh
⇩
Reck
⇩
Reckless
⇩
I was reckless
⇩
I was reckless when I was younger.

PEACHIE SPEECHIE'S
R SOUND CHAINING

/ɛr/

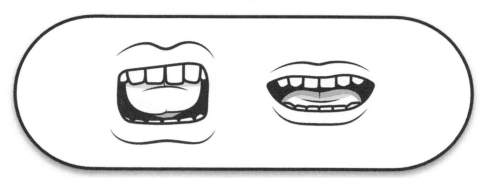

Reh

⇩

Rel

⇩

Relish

⇩

Want relish

⇩

Do you want relish on your hot dog?

PEACHIE SPEECHIE'S
R SOUND CHAINING

/ɝ/

Reh
⇩
Rep
⇩
Reptile
⇩
Reptile exhibit
⇩
Did you see the reptile exhibit at the zoo?

PEACHIE SPEECHIE'S
R SOUND CHAINING

/ɝ/

Reh
⇩
Reck
⇩
Recommend
⇩
Recommend the book
⇩
Would you recommend the book to a friend?

PEACHIE SPEECHIE'S
R SOUND CHAINING

/ɝ/

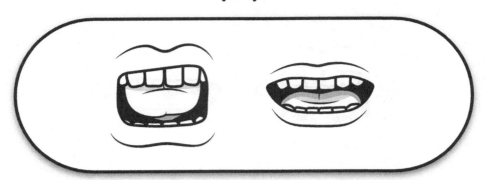

Reh
⇩
Reck
⇩
Rectangle
⇩
Paint a rectangle
⇩
I will paint a rectangle on this paper.

PEACHIE SPEECHIE'S
R SOUND CHAINING

/ɝ/

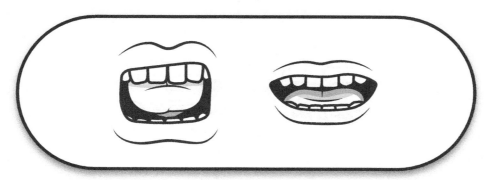

Reh
⇩
Res
⇩
Resolution
⇩
Find a resolution
⇩
Did you find a resolution to the problem?

PEACHIE SPEECHIE'S
R SOUND CHAINING

/ɝ/

Reh
⇩
Rect
⇩
Correct
⇩
Correct choice
⇩
Did you make the correct choice?

PEACHIE SPEECHIE'S
R SOUND CHAINING

/ɹɛ/

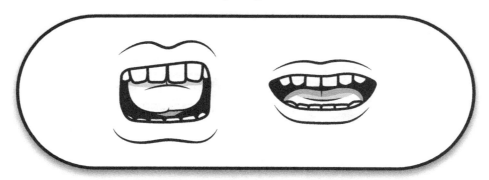

Reh
⇩
Ress
⇩
Recipe
⇩
New recipe
⇩
Have you tried the new recipe yet?

PEACHIE SPEECHIE'S
R SOUND CHAINING

/ɜr/

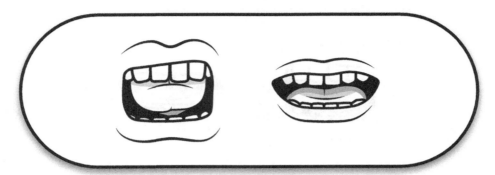

Reh
⇩
Reb
⇩
Rebel
⇩
She's a rebel
⇩
She's a rebel who makes her own rules.

PEACHIE SPEECHIE'S
R SOUND CHAINING

/ɹɛ/

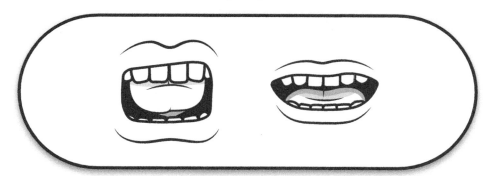

Reh
⇩
Red
⇩
Ready
⇩
Ready for lunch
⇩
Is he ready for lunch yet?

PEACHIE SPEECHIE'S
R SOUND CHAINING

/ɹæ/

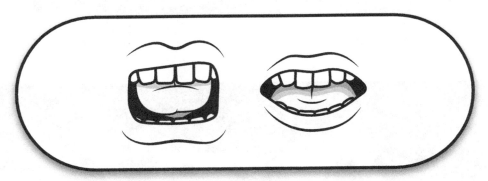

Ra
⇩
Rack
⇩
Racket
⇩
Tennis racket
⇩
I bought a new tennis racket.

PEACHIE SPEECHIE'S
R SOUND CHAINING

/ɹæ/

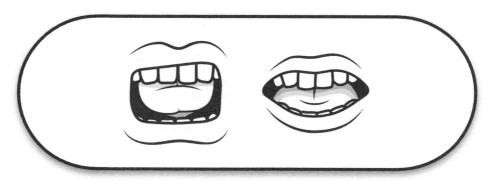

Ra

⇩

Wrap

⇩

Wrapping

⇩

Wrapping a gift

⇩

I'm wrapping a gift for the big party tonight.

PEACHIE SPEECHIE'S
R SOUND CHAINING

/ɹæ/

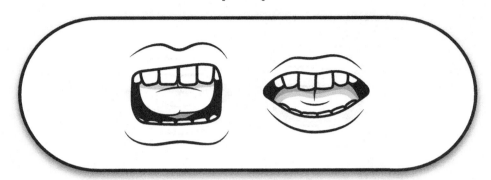

Ra
⇩
Rag
⇩
Ragged
⇩
Ragged coat
⇩
He loved his old ragged coat.

Peachie Speechie's
R Sound Chaining

/ɹæ/

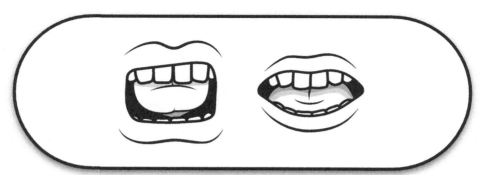

Ra
⇩
Rat
⇩
Rattle
⇩
Baby's rattle
⇩
She is shaking the baby's rattle.

PEACHIE SPEECHIE'S
R SOUND CHAINING

/ɹæ/

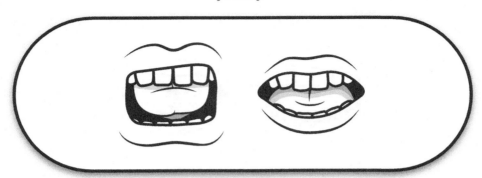

Ra
⇩
Raz
⇩
Razzle
⇩
Razzle dazzle
⇩
The magician used a little razzle-dazzle to entertain us.

PEACHIE SPEECHIE'S
R SOUND CHAINING

/ɹæ/

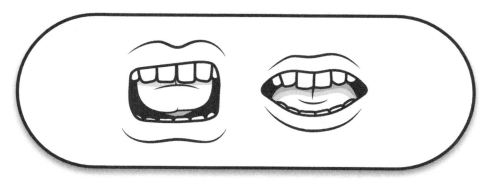

Ra

⇩

Rab

⇩

Rabbi

⇩

Saw the rabbi

⇩

We saw the rabbi last week.

PEACHIE SPEECHIE'S
R SOUND CHAINING

/ɹæ/

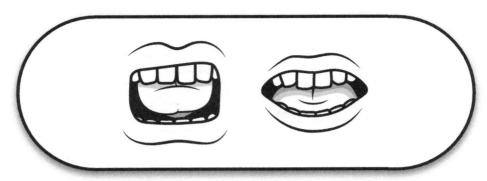

Ra

⇩

Rad

⇩

Radical

⇩

Radical idea

⇩

It's not exactly a radical idea.

PEACHIE SPEECHIE'S
R SOUND CHAINING

/ɹæ/

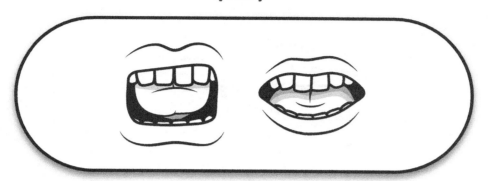

Ra
⇩
Rack
⇩
Raccoon
⇩
Baby raccoon
⇩
I saw a baby raccoon outside.

PEACHIE SPEECHIE'S
R SOUND CHAINING

/ɹæ/

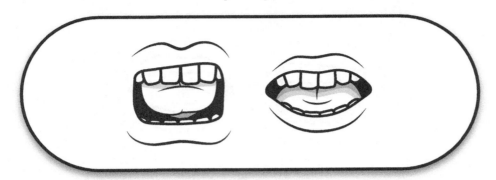

Ra
⇩
Rad
⇩
Radish
⇩
Radish salad
⇩
My dad made a radish salad.

R SOUND CHAINING

/ɹæ/

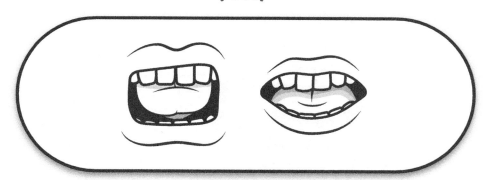

Ra
⇩
Raff
⇩
Raffle
⇩
Won the raffle
⇩
I won the raffle at school.

PEACHIE SPEECHIE'S
R SOUND CHAINING

/ɹæ/

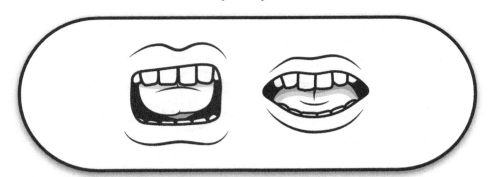

Ra
⇩
Rap
⇩
Rapidly
⇩
Moved rapidly
⇩
The train moved rapidly along the track.

PEACHIE SPEECHIE'S
R SOUND CHAINING

/ɹæ/

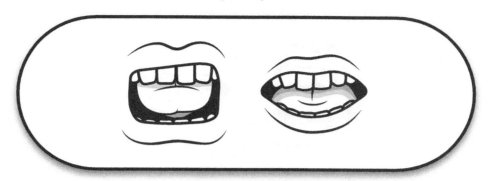

Ra
⇩
Rach
⇩
Rachet
⇩
Has a rachet
⇩
Dad has a rachet in his toolbox.

PEACHIE SPEECHIE'S
R SOUND CHAINING

/ɹæ/

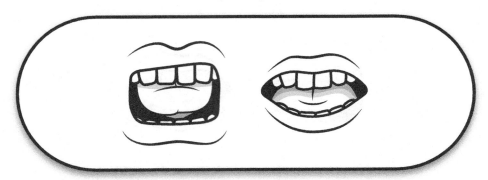

Ra
⇩
Rash
⇩
Rational
⇩
Rational decision
⇩
That was a rational decision.

Peachie Speechie's
R Sound Chaining

/ɹæ/

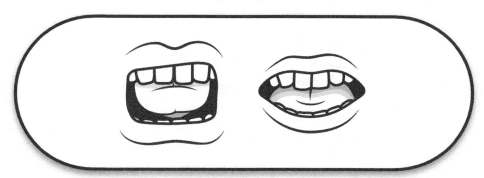

Ra
⇩
Rav
⇩
Ravenous
⇩
Was ravenous
⇩
I was ravenous after the big race.

PEACHIE SPEECHIE'S
R SOUND CHAINING

/ɹæ/

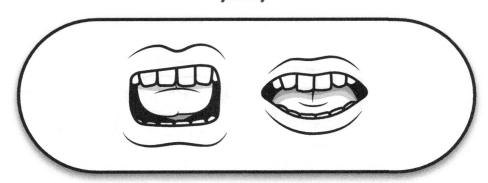

Ra

Rack

Racquetball

Play racquetball

Do you want to play racquetball with me?

PEACHIE SPEECHIE'S
R SOUND CHAINING

/ɹæ/

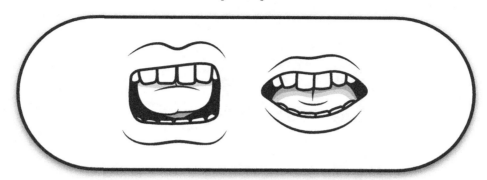

Ra
⇩
Rav
⇩
Unravel
⇩
Unravel the knots
⇩
The kids tried to unravel the knots.

PEACHIE SPEECHIE'S
R SOUND CHAINING

/ɹæ/

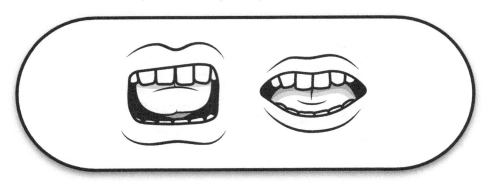

Ra
⇩
Raff
⇩
Giraffe
⇩
Tall giraffe
⇩
The tall giraffe was eating leaves

PEACHIE SPEECHIE'S
R SOUND CHAINING

/ɹæ/

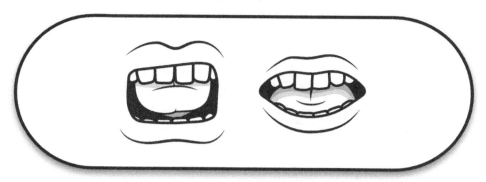

Ra

⇩

Ral

⇩

Corral

⇩

In the corral

⇩

The donkeys waited in the corral.

Peachie Speechie's
R Sound Chaining

/ɹæ/

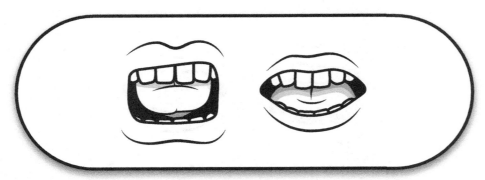

Ra

⇩

Ran

⇩

Rancid

⇩

It was rancid

⇩

We threw away the milk because it was rancid.

Peachie Speechie's
R SOUND CHAINING

/ɹæ/

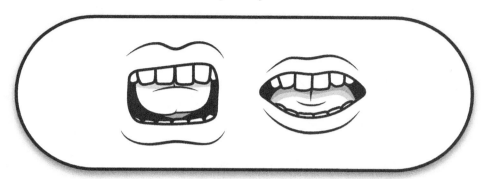

Ra
⇩
Ran
⇩
Randomly
⇩
Randomly chosen
⇩
I was randomly chosen to be in the show.

PEACHIE SPEECHIE'S
R SOUND CHAINING

/ɹu/

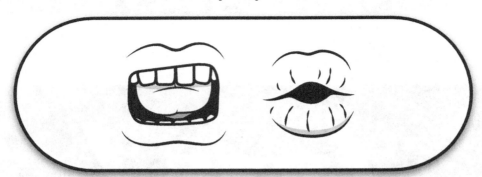

Roo
⇩
Room
⇩
Rooming
⇩
Rooming together
⇩
Are we rooming together at camp?

PEACHIE SPEECHIE'S
R SOUND CHAINING

/ɹu/

Roo
⇩
Roof
⇩
Roofing
⇩
Roofing company
⇩
The roofing company is coming out to fix the leak.

PEACHIE SPEECHIE'S
R SOUND CHAINING

/ɹu/

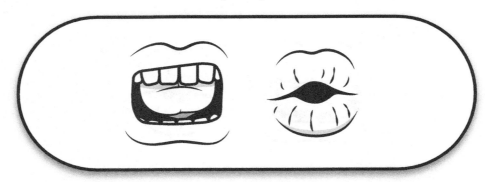

Roo

⇩

Root

⇩

Rooting

⇩

Rooting around

⇩

The chipmunk was rooting around the yard for a snack.

PEACHIE SPEECHIE'S
R SOUND CHAINING

/ɹu/

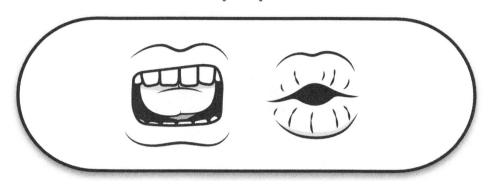

Roo
⇩
Rude
⇩
Rudolph
⇩
Rudolph pulled.
⇩
Rudolph pulled the sleigh.

PEACHIE SPEECHIE'S
R SOUND CHAINING

/ɹu/

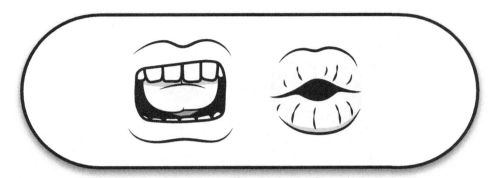

Roo
⇩
Rule
⇩
Ruling
⇩
He is ruling
⇩
He is ruling the kingdom.

PEACHIE SPEECHIE'S
R SOUND CHAINING

/ɹu/

Roo
⇩
Ruth
⇩
Ruthless
⇩
Ruthless in battle
⇩
The viking was ruthless in battle.

Peachie Speechie's
R Sound Chaining

/ɹu/

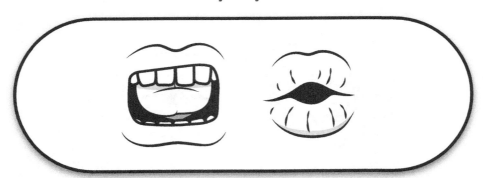

Roo
⇩
Roob
⇩
Ruby
⇩
Ruby Falls
⇩
Have you visited Ruby Falls?

PEACHIE SPEECHIE'S
R SOUND CHAINING

/ɹu/

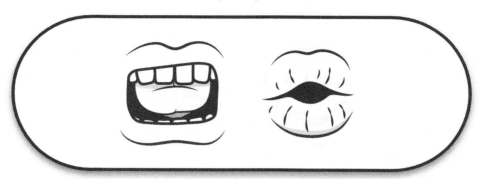

Roo
⇩
Room
⇩
Bedroom
⇩
My bedroom
⇩
I'm going to take a nap in my bedroom.

PEACHIE SPEECHIE'S
R SOUND CHAINING

/ɹu/

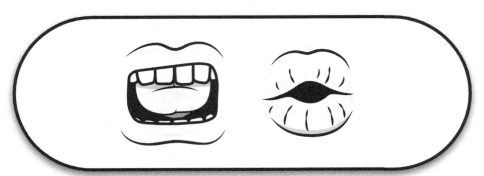

Roo
⇩
Root
⇩
Rooting
⇩
Rooting for you
⇩
I will be rooting for you.

PEACHIE SPEECHIE'S
R SOUND CHAINING

/ɹu/

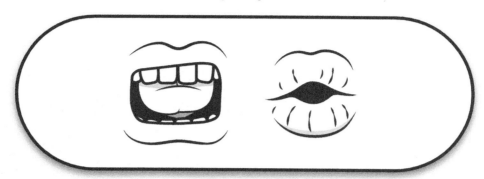

Roo
⇩
Rube
⇩
Aruba
⇩
Been to Aruba
⇩
Have you been to Aruba?

PEACHIE SPEECHIE'S
R SOUND CHAINING

/ɹʌ/

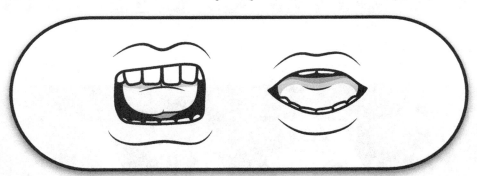

Ruh
⇩
Ruff
⇩
Ruffled
⇩
Ruffled his feathers
⇩
The bird squawked and ruffled his feathers.

PEACHIE SPEECHIE'S
R SOUND CHAINING

/ɹʌ/

Ruh
⇩
Rum
⇩
Rummy
⇩
Play rummy
⇩
I like to play rummy with my friends.

PEACHIE SPEECHIE'S
R SOUND CHAINING

/ɹʌ/

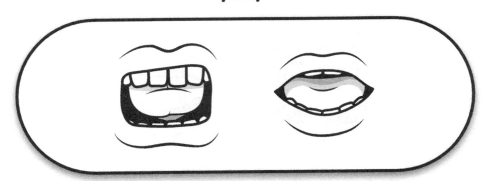

Ruh
⇩
Run
⇩
Running
⇩
Running fast
⇩
He was running fast through the field.

Peachie Speechie's
R SOUND CHAINING

/ɹʌ/

Ruh
⇩
Rub
⇩
Rubbing
⇩
Rubbing lotion
⇩
She is rubbing lotion on her hands.

PEACHIE SPEECHIE'S
R SOUND CHAINING

/ɹʌ/

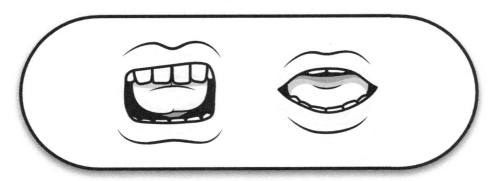

Ruh
⇩
Rush
⇩
Rushing
⇩
Rushing through
⇩
I was rushing through my work and made a mistake.

PEACHIE SPEECHIE'S
R SOUND CHAINING

/ɹʌ/

Ruh
⇩
Ruff
⇩
Ruffles
⇩
Blue ruffles
⇩
She had blue ruffles on her dress.

Peachie Speechie's R SOUND CHAINING

/ɹʌ/

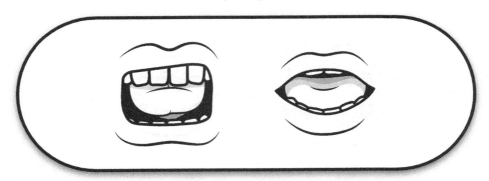

Ruh

⇩

Rum

⇩

Rummaging

⇩

Rummaging through

⇩

The raccoon was rummaging through the trash can.

PEACHIE SPEECHIE'S
R SOUND CHAINING

/ɹʌ/

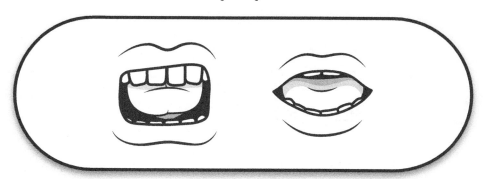

Ruh
⇩
Rust
⇩
Rustic
⇩
Rustic cabin
⇩
We stayed in a rustic cabin last summer.

PEACHIE SPEECHIE'S
R SOUND CHAINING

/ɹʌ/

Ruh
⇩
Rush
⇩
Russia
⇩
Capital of Russia
⇩
Moscow is the capital of Russia.

PEACHIE SPEECHIE'S
R SOUND CHAINING

/ɹʌ/

Ruh
⇩
Run
⇩
Runaway
⇩
Runaway success
⇩
The school play was a runaway success.

PEACHIE SPEECHIE'S
R SOUND CHAINING

/ɹʌ/

Ruh
⇩
Rug
⇩
Rugged
⇩
Rugged path
⇩
We climbed the rugged path.

PEACHIE SPEECHIE'S
R SOUND CHAINING

/ɝ/

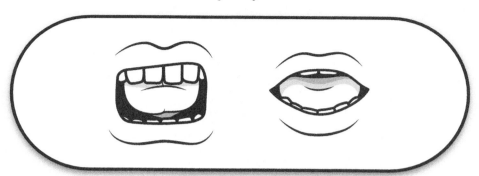

Ruh
⇩
Russ
⇩
Russell
⇩
Uncle Russell
⇩
My uncle Russell is an excellent swimmer.

Peachie Speechie's R SOUND CHAINING

/raɪ/

rye

PEACHIE SPEECHIE'S
R SOUND CHAINING

/ɹaɪ/

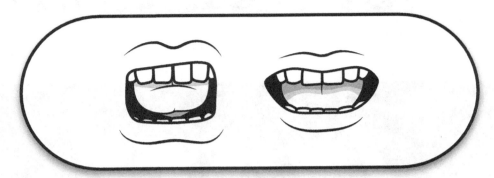

Rye
⇩
Rhyme
⇩
Rhyming
⇩
Rhyming words
⇩
They learned about rhyming words at school.

PEACHIE SPEECHIE'S
R SOUND CHAINING

/ɹaɪ/

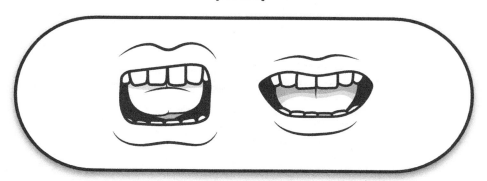

Rye
⇩
Ride
⇩
Riding
⇩
Riding bikes
⇩
We are riding bikes in the park.

PEACHIE SPEECHIE'S
R SOUND CHAINING

/ɹaɪ/

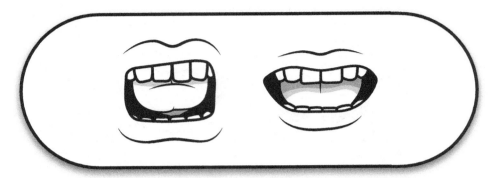

Rye
⇩
Ripe
⇩
Ripen
⇩
Will ripen
⇩
The apples will ripen in autumn.

PEACHIE SPEECHIE'S
R SOUND CHAINING

/ɹaɪ/

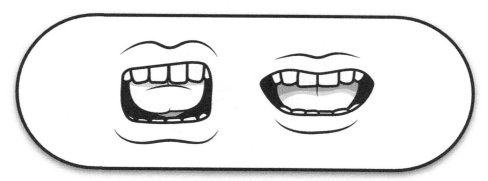

Rye
⇩
Rive
⇩
Arrive
⇩
Will arrive soon
⇩
The guests will arrive soon.

Peachie Speechie's R Sound Chaining

/ɹaɪ/

Rye

⇩

Write

⇩

Writing

⇩

Writing assignment

⇩

I am done with my writing assignment.

PEACHIE SPEECHIE'S
R SOUND CHAINING

/ɹaɪ/

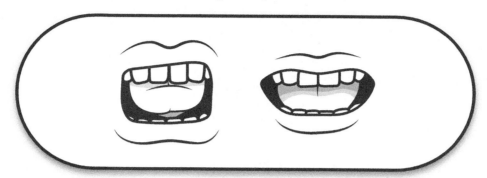

Rye
⇩
Rise
⇩
Rising
⇩
Sun is rising
⇩
The sun is rising in the sky.

PEACHIE SPEECHIE'S
R SOUND CHAINING

PEACHIE SPEECHIE'S
R SOUND CHAINING

/dɹ/

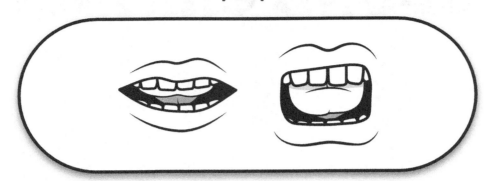

Dr
⇩
Drum
⇩
Drumming
⇩
Drumming loudly
⇩
He is drumming loudly in the basement.

PEACHIE SPEECHIE'S
R SOUND CHAINING

/dɹ/

Dr
⇩
Drink
⇩
Drinking
⇩
Drinking straw
⇩
I need a drinking straw for my smoothie.

PEACHIE SPEECHIE'S
R SOUND CHAINING

/dɹ/

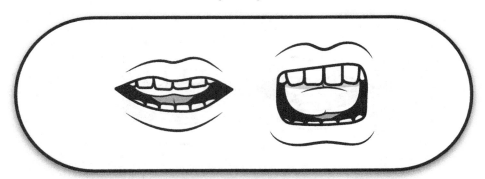

Dr
⇩
Drop
⇩
Dropping
⇩
Dropping by today
⇩
My uncle is dropping by today for a visit.

Peachie Speechie's R Sound Chaining

/dɹ/

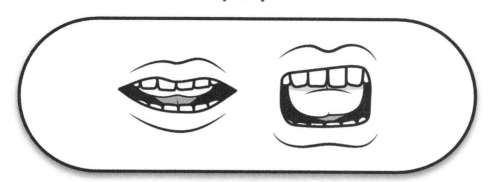

Dr
⇩
Drone
⇩
Droning
⇩
Droning on and on
⇩
They were droning on and on about the homework.

PEACHIE SPEECHIE'S
R SOUND CHAINING

/dɹ/

Dr

Dre

Dreidel

Spin the dreidel
⇩
Spin the dreidel on the table.

PEACHIE SPEECHIE'S
R SOUND CHAINING

/dɹ/

Dr
⇩
Draft
⇩
Drafty
⇩
Cool and drafty
⇩
It feels cool and drafty in here.

Peachie Speechie's R Sound Chaining

/dɹ/

Dr
⇩
Dream
⇩
Dreaming
⇩
I am dreaming
⇩
I am dreaming of a relaxing vacation.

PEACHIE SPEECHIE'S
R SOUND CHAINING

/dɹ/

Dr
⇩
Dress
⇩
Dressing
⇩
Salad dressing
⇩
Put some salad dressing on it.

PEACHIE SPEECHIE'S
R SOUND CHAINING

/dɹ/

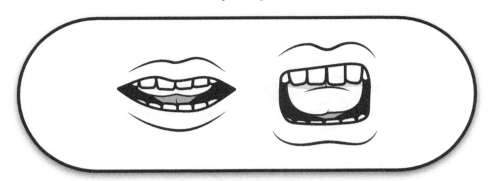

Dr
⇩
Drip
⇩
Dripping
⇩
Has been dripping
⇩
The faucet has been dripping all night.

Peachie Speechie's
R Sound Chaining

/dɹ/

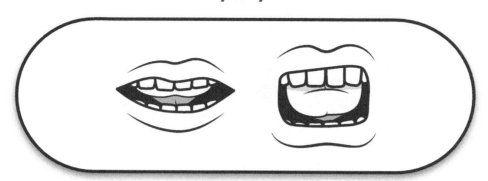

Dr
⇩
Drag
⇩
Dragon
⇩
Big dragon
⇩
The big dragon was gentle.

PEACHIE SPEECHIE'S
R SOUND CHAINING

/dɹ/

Dr

⇩

Draw

⇩

Drawing

⇩

Drawing a picture

⇩

I'm drawing a picture of a cat.

Peachie Speechie's
R Sound Chaining

/dɹ/

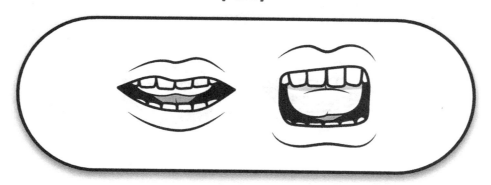

Dr
⇩
Drive
⇩
Driving
⇩
Driving away
⇩
She was driving away from the house.

PEACHIE SPEECHIE'S
R SOUND CHAINING

/dɹ/

Dr

⇩

Droop

⇩

Droopy

⇩

Droopy ears

⇩

The puppy had cute droopy ears.

PEACHIE SPEECHIE'S
R SOUND CHAINING

/dɹ/

Dr
⇩
Dress
⇩
Address
⇩
New address
⇩
What is your new address?

PEACHIE SPEECHIE'S
R SOUND CHAINING

/dɹ/

Dr
⇩
Droo
⇩
Drooling
⇩
Dog is drooling
⇩
The dog is drooling on the couch.

PEACHIE SPEECHIE'S
R SOUND CHAINING

/dɹ/

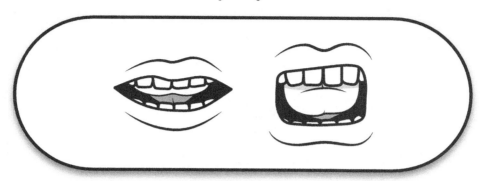

Dr
⇩
Dread
⇩
Dreading
⇩
Have been dreading
⇩
I have been dreading this all afternoon.

PEACHIE SPEECHIE'S
R SOUND CHAINING

PEACHIE SPEECHIE'S
R SOUND CHAINING

/tɹ/

Tr

⇩

Trip

⇩

Tripping

⇩

Tripping over them

⇩

My shoes were too big, so I was tripping over them.

PEACHIE SPEECHIE'S
R SOUND CHAINING

/tɹ/

Tr

⇩

Trust

⇩

Trustworthy

⇩

Trustworthy friend

⇩

It's good to have such a kind and trustworthy friend.

Peachie Speechie's
R Sound Chaining

/tɹ/

Tr
⇩
Trend
⇩
Trending
⇩
What's trending
⇩
What's trending on social media right now?

PEACHIE SPEECHIE'S
R SOUND CHAINING

/tɹ/

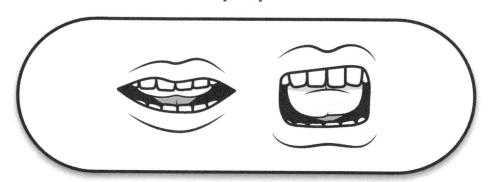

Tr

⇩

Trick

⇩

Tricky

⇩

Tricky problem

⇩

We had a tricky problem on the math test.

Peachie Speechie's R Sound Chaining

/tɹ/

Tr

⇩

Tread

⇩

Treading

⇩

Treading water

⇩

They are treading water in the pool.

PEACHIE SPEECHIE'S
R SOUND CHAINING

/tɹ/

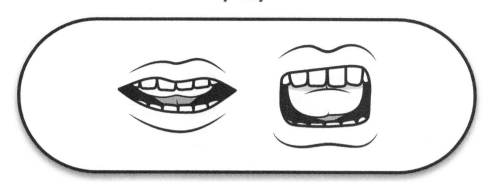

Tr

⇩

Trace

⇩

Tracing

⇩

Tracing the lines

⇩

She is tracing the lines on the worksheet.

PEACHIE SPEECHIE'S
R SOUND CHAINING

/tɹ/

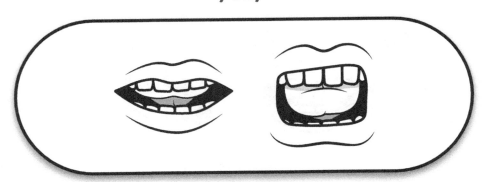

Tr
⇩
Track
⇩
Tracking
⇩
Tracking device
⇩
I put a tracking device on my cat.

PEACHIE SPEECHIE'S
R SOUND CHAINING

/tɹ/

Tr

⇩

Trim

⇩

Trimming

⇩

Trimming the bushes

⇩

He is trimming the bushes in the yard.

PEACHIE SPEECHIE'S
R SOUND CHAINING

/tɹ/

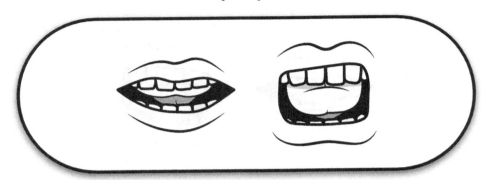

Tr

Trade

Trading

Trading snacks

We are trading snacks at lunch.

Peachie Speechie's
R Sound Chaining

/tɹ/

Tr

⇩

Try

⇩

Trying

⇩

Keep trying

⇩

I keep trying to win the game.

PEACHIE SPEECHIE'S
R SOUND CHAINING

/tɹ/

Tr
⇩
Train
⇩
Training
⇩
Dog training school
⇩
We sent my puppy to a dog training school.

PEACHIE SPEECHIE'S
R SOUND CHAINING

/tɹ/

Tr

⇩

Trop

⇩

Tropical

⇩

Tropical island

⇩

I want to visit a tropical island.

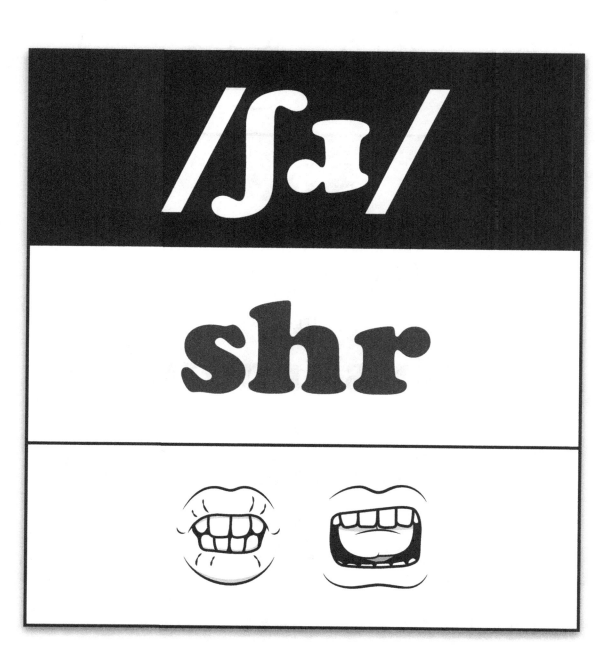

PEACHIE SPEECHIE'S
R SOUND CHAINING

/ʃɹ/

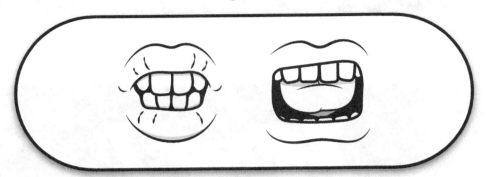

Shr
⇩
Shroom
⇩
Mushroom
⇩
Mushroom pizza
⇩
I want a thin crust mushroom pizza.

PEACHIE SPEECHIE'S
R SOUND CHAINING

/ʃɹ/

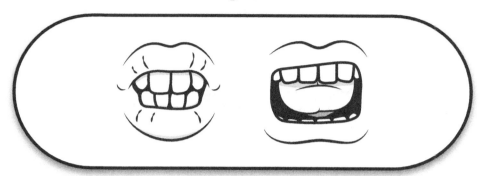

Shr
⇩
Shriek
⇩
Shrieking
⇩
Was shrieking loudly
⇩
She was shrieking loudly after seeing the mouse.

PEACHIE SPEECHIE'S
R SOUND CHAINING

/ʃɹ/

Shr

⇩

Shrag

⇩

Dishrag

⇩

Put the dishrag

⇩

Please put the dishrag in the sink.

PEACHIE SPEECHIE'S
R SOUND CHAINING

/ʃɹ/

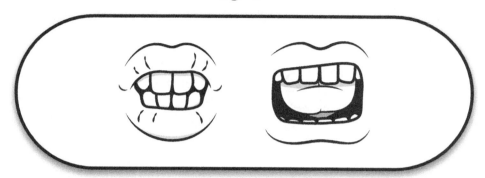

Shr

⇩

Shrink

⇩

Shrinking

⇩

Magic shrinking powder

⇩

The wizard had magic shrinking powder.

Peachie Speechie's
R Sound Chaining

/ʃɹ/

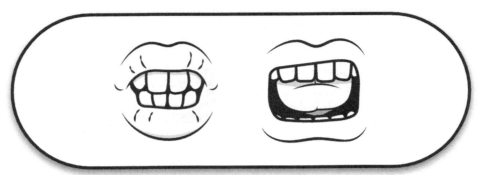

Shr
⇩
Shrug
⇩
Shrugging
⇩
Was shrugging
⇩
He was shrugging his shoulders.

PEACHIE SPEECHIE'S
R SOUND CHAINING

/ʃɹ/

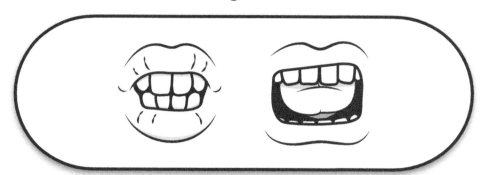

Shr
⇩
Shred
⇩
Shredding
⇩
Shredding paper
⇩
They are shredding paper in the office today.

PEACHIE SPEECHIE'S
R SOUND CHAINING

R SOUND CHAINING
by Peachie Speechie

Directions: Start by saying the first utterance in the chain several times. Then, move to the next utterance in the chain. They become longer and more complex as you go.

BONUS: Can you make up your own sentences using the bolded phrases below?

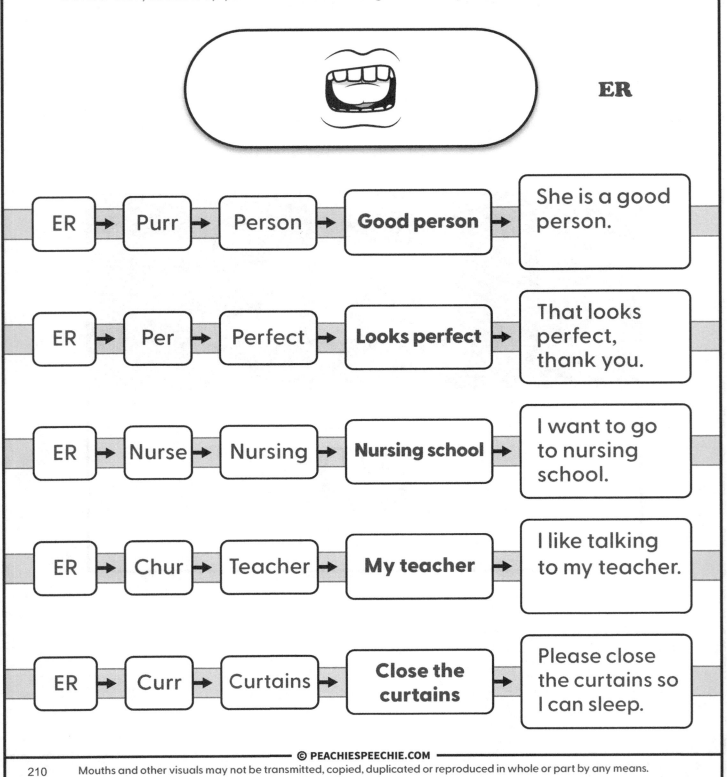

ER

ER → Purr → Person → **Good person** → She is a good person.

ER → Per → Perfect → **Looks perfect** → That looks perfect, thank you.

ER → Nurse → Nursing → **Nursing school** → I want to go to nursing school.

ER → Chur → Teacher → **My teacher** → I like talking to my teacher.

ER → Curr → Curtains → **Close the curtains** → Please close the curtains so I can sleep.

© PEACHIESPEECHIE.COM

Peachie Speechie's R Sound Chaining

ER

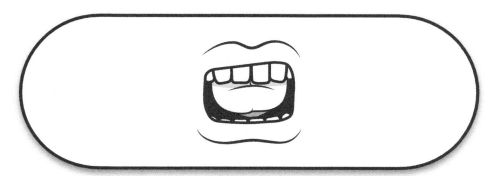

Her
⇩
Hurt
⇩
Hurting
⇩
Foot hurting
⇩
Why is my foot hurting?

PEACHIE SPEECHIE'S
R SOUND CHAINING

ER

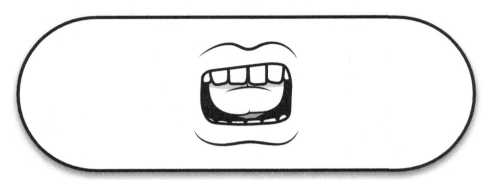

Her
⇩
Heard
⇩
Hurdle
⇩
The hurdle
⇩
Jump over the hurdle.

PEACHIE SPEECHIE'S
R SOUND CHAINING

ER

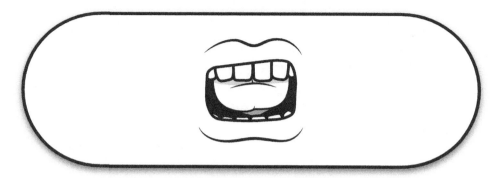

Fir

⇩

Firm

⇩

Confirm

⇩

Confirm it

⇩

Please confirm it with the front office.

PEACHIE SPEECHIE'S
R SOUND CHAINING

ER

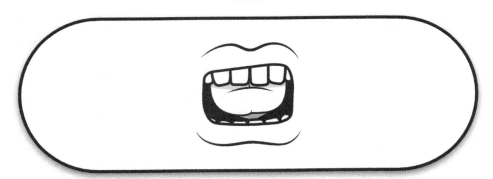

Fir
⇩
Fern
⇩
Furnace
⇩
Old furnace
⇩
The old furnace is in the basement.

Peachie Speechie's
R Sound Chaining

ER

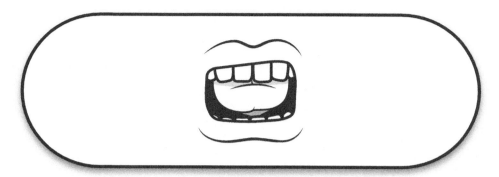

Burr
⇩
Bird
⇩
Birdcage
⇩
In the birdcage
⇩
Tweety is in the birdcage.

PEACHIE SPEECHIE'S
R SOUND CHAINING

ER

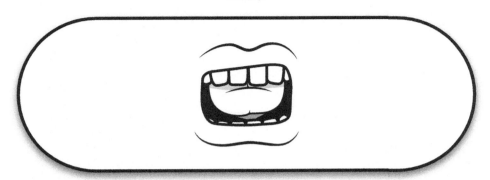

Burr
⇩
Birth
⇩
Birthday
⇩
Birthday cake
⇩
I had a vanilla birthday cake.

PEACHIE SPEECHIE'S
R SOUND CHAINING

ER

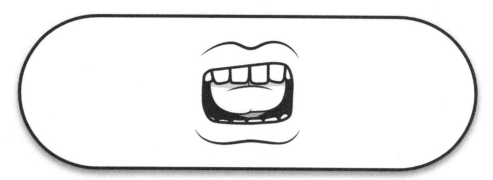

Burr
⇩
Burn
⇩
Burning
⇩
Burning food
⇩
It smells like you're burning food in the oven.

PEACHIE SPEECHIE'S
R SOUND CHAINING

ER

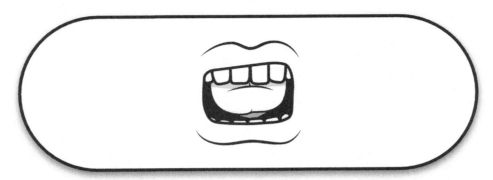

Were

⇩

Word

⇩

Password

⇩

My password

⇩

I won't tell you my password.

Peachie Speechie's
R Sound Chaining

ER

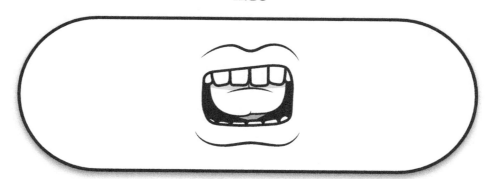

Were

Work

Working

I'm working

I'm working on a project today.

Peachie Speechie's
R Sound Chaining

ER

Were
⇩
Worm
⇩
Bookworm
⇩
Is a bookworm
⇩
Everyone says my mom is a bookworm.

R SOUND CHAINING

ER

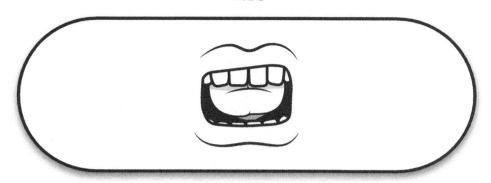

Were

⇩

Werz

⇩

Flowers

⇩

Beautiful flowers

⇩

I love this bouquet of beautiful flowers.

PEACHIE SPEECHIE'S
R SOUND CHAINING

ER

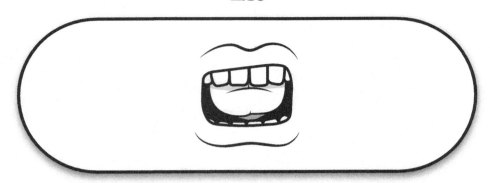

Purr

⇩

Perm

⇩

Permanent

⇩

Permanent ink

⇩

The permanent ink stained the couch.

PEACHIE SPEECHIE'S
R SOUND CHAINING

ER

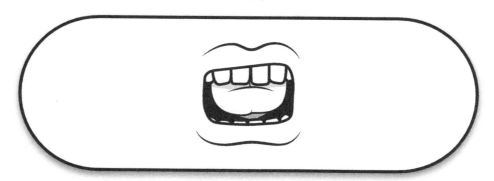

Per
⇩
Perch
⇩
Purchase
⇩
Big purchase
⇩
My car was a big purchase.

PEACHIE SPEECHIE'S
R SOUND CHAINING

ER

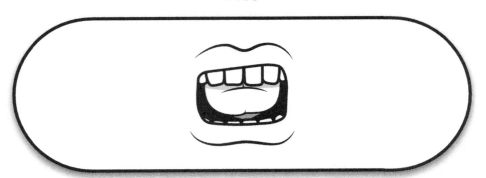

Turr
⇩
Turn
⇩
Turning
⇩
Turning left
⇩
I will be turning left at the light.

PEACHIE SPEECHIE'S
R SOUND CHAINING

ER

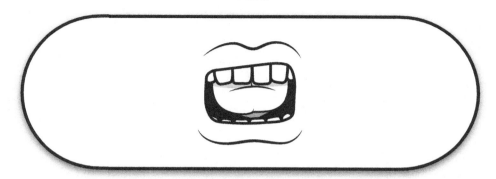

Burr

⇩

Burrs

⇩

Numbers

⇩

See the numbers

⇩

Did you see the numbers on the chart?

PEACHIE SPEECHIE'S
R SOUND CHAINING

ER

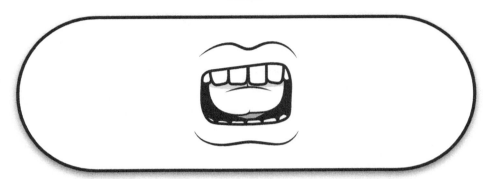

Nurr
⇩
Nurse
⇩
Nursing
⇩
Nursing school
⇩
My cousin went to nursing school.

Peachie Speechie's R Sound Chaining

ER

Ker

⇩

Kerz

⇩

Sneakers

⇩

New sneakers

⇩

Did you see those new sneakers?

PEACHIE SPEECHIE'S
R SOUND CHAINING

ER

Chur
⇩
Churz
⇩
Teachers
⇩
Two teachers
⇩
I have two teachers in my class.

PEACHIE SPEECHIE'S
R SOUND CHAINING

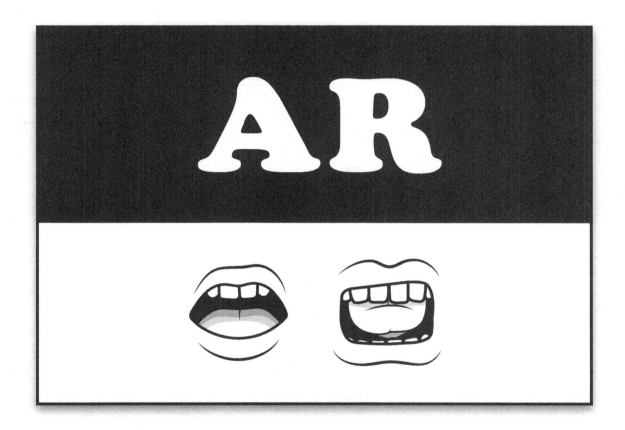

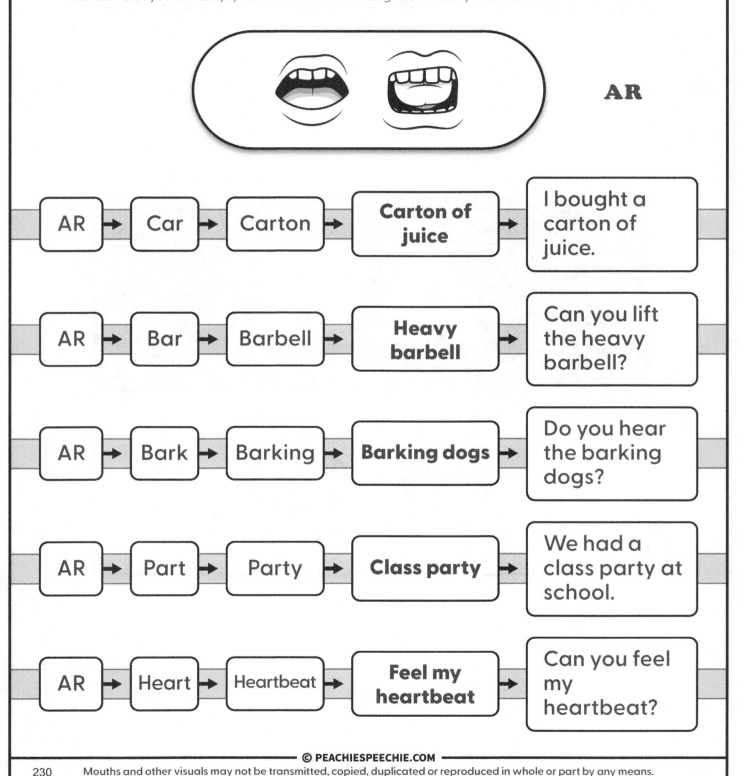

PEACHIE SPEECHIE'S
R SOUND CHAINING

AR

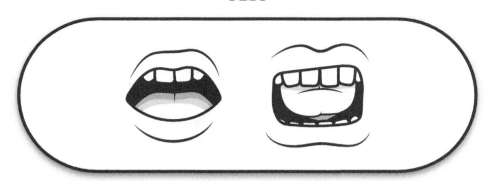

Ar

⇩

Par

⇩

Party

⇩

Birthday party

⇩

Will you come to my birthday party?

PEACHIE SPEECHIE'S
R SOUND CHAINING

AR

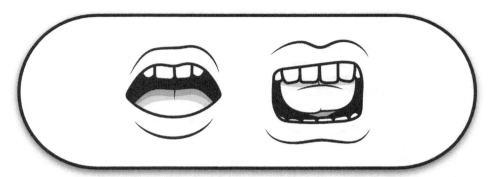

Ar
⇩
Char
⇩
Charcoal
⇩
Add charcoal
⇩
Did you add charcoal to the grill?

PEACHIE SPEECHIE'S
R SOUND CHAINING

AR

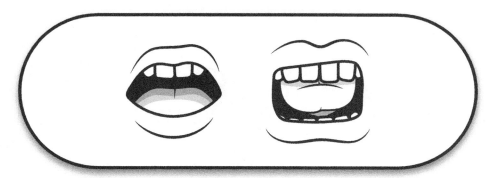

Ar
⇩
Sar
⇩
Sorry
⇩
I'm so sorry
⇩
I'm so sorry about that.

PEACHIE SPEECHIE'S
R SOUND CHAINING

AR

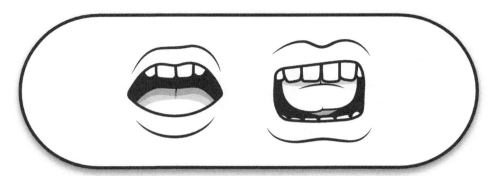

Ar
⇩
Ark
⇩
Arkansas
⇩
Visit Arkansas
⇩
Do you want to visit Arkansas?

PEACHIE SPEECHIE'S
R SOUND CHAINING

AR

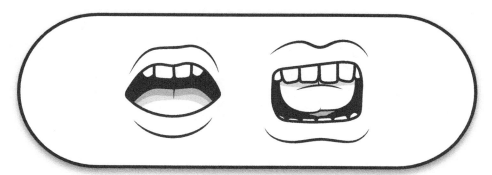

Ar
⇩
Car
⇩
Carpet
⇩
Magic carpet
⇩
They flew on a magic carpet.

PEACHIE SPEECHIE'S
R SOUND CHAINING

AR

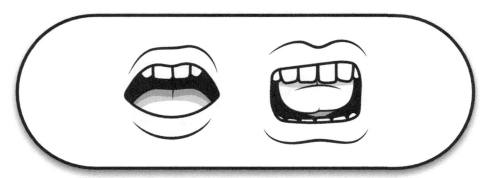

Ar
⇩
Mark
⇩
Market
⇩
To the market
⇩
We went to the market today.

Peachie Speechie's R Sound Chaining

AR

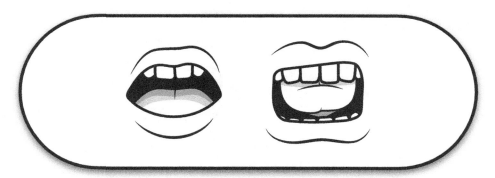

Ar
⇩
Farm
⇩
Farming
⇩
Been farming
⇩
I've been farming since I was a child.

PEACHIE SPEECHIE'S
R SOUND CHAINING

AR

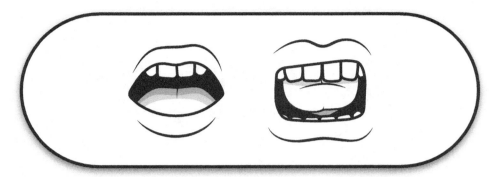

Ar
⇩
Tar
⇩
Target
⇩
Go to Target
⇩
Do you want to go to Target?

PEACHIE SPEECHIE'S
R SOUND CHAINING

AR

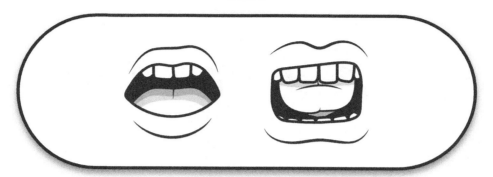

Ar
⇩
Par
⇩
Parking
⇩
Parking spot
⇩
I'm looking for a parking spot.

PEACHIE SPEECHIE'S
R SOUND CHAINING

AR

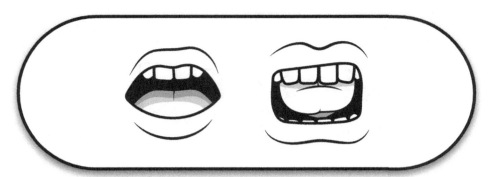

Ar
⇩
March
⇩
Marching
⇩
Marching band
⇩
Will you join the marching band?

PEACHIE SPEECHIE'S
R SOUND CHAINING

AR

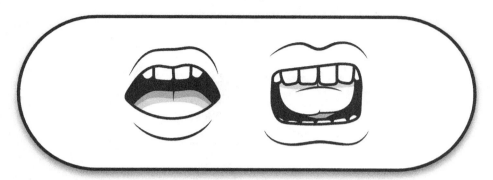

Ar
⇩
Dark
⇩
Darkest
⇩
Darkest night
⇩
It was the darkest night of the year.

Peachie Speechie's R Sound Chaining

AR

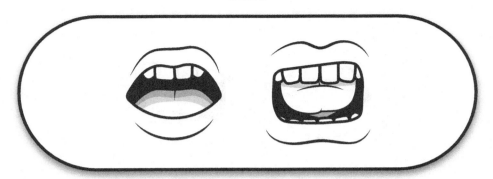

Ar
⇩
Charge
⇩
Charging
⇩
Charging the phone
⇩
You should be charging the phone at night.

Peachie Speechie's
R Sound Chaining

AR

Ar
⇩
Cart
⇩
Go-Cart
⇩
Drive a go-cart
⇩
Do you know how to drive a go-cart?

PEACHIE SPEECHIE'S
R SOUND CHAINING

AR

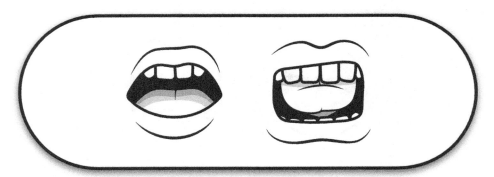

Ar
⇩
Arm
⇩
Alarm
⇩
Alarm clock
⇩
Set the alarm clock for 7:15am.

PEACHIE SPEECHIE'S
R SOUND CHAINING

AR

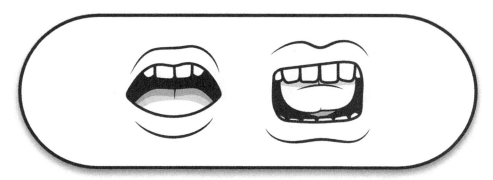

Ar
⇩
Bark
⇩
Barking
⇩
Barking loudly
⇩
The little dog is barking loudly.

Peachie Speechie's
R Sound Chaining

AR

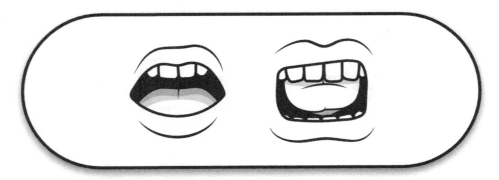

Ar

⇩

Car

⇩

Carnival

⇩

Holiday carnival

⇩

Will you be at the holiday carnival?

Peachie Speechie's R SOUND CHAINING

AR

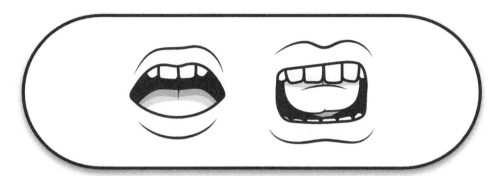

Ar

⇩

Far

⇩

Farting

⇩

Dog was farting

⇩

My dog was farting last night.

PEACHIE SPEECHIE'S
R SOUND CHAINING

AR

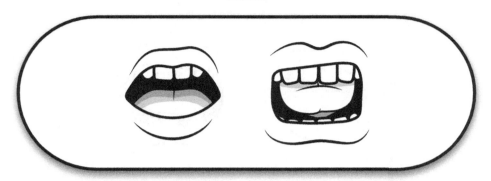

Ar
⇩
Heart
⇩
Heartbeat
⇩
The baby's heartbeat
⇩
She listened to the baby's heartbeat.

PEACHIE SPEECHIE'S
R SOUND CHAINING

AR

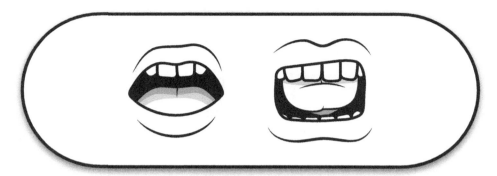

Ar
⇩
Gar
⇩
Garlic
⇩
Put garlic
⇩
Did you put garlic in the soup?

PEACHIE SPEECHIE'S
R SOUND CHAINING

AR

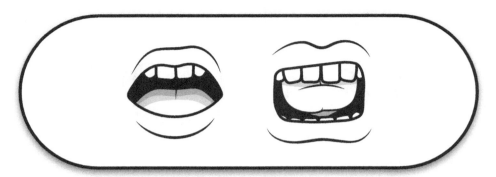

Ar
⇩
Spar
⇩
Sparkling
⇩
Sparkling lights
⇩
Look at the sparkling lights outside.

PEACHIE SPEECHIE'S
R SOUND CHAINING

AR

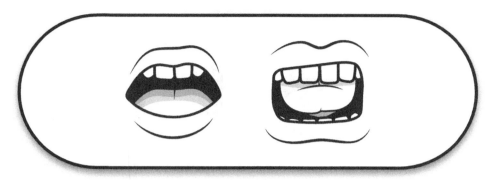

Ar
⇩
Mar
⇩
Marbles
⇩
Glass marbles
⇩
I have a collection of glass marbles.

PEACHIE SPEECHIE'S
R SOUND CHAINING

AR

Ar

⇩

Gar

⇩

Garbage

⇩

Garbage can

⇩

Put that stuff in the garbage can.

PEACHIE SPEECHIE'S
R SOUND CHAINING

AR

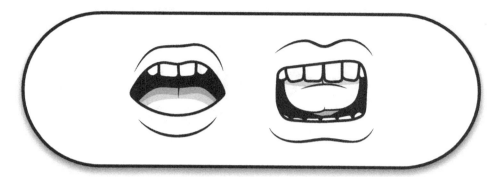

Ar

⇩

Ark

⇩

Architect

⇩

Famous architect

⇩

A famous architect designed this building.

Peachie Speechie's
R Sound Chaining

AR

Ar

⇩

Arm

⇩

Army

⇩

Strong army

⇩

We have a strong army to protect us.

PEACHIE SPEECHIE'S
R SOUND CHAINING

AR

Ar

⇩

Art

⇩

Artwork

⇩

Children's artwork

⇩

Did you see the children's artwork at school?

PEACHIE SPEECHIE'S
R SOUND CHAINING

AR

Ar

Car

Carton

Carton of milk

The carton of milk is in the fridge.

Peachie Speechie's R SOUND CHAINING

AR

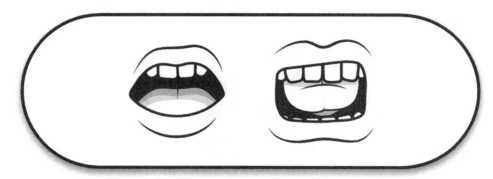

Ar

⇩

Bar

⇩

Barfing

⇩

Barfing all night

⇩

She got food poisoning and was barfing all night.

Peachie Speechie's
R Sound Chaining

AR

Ar

Tar

Tarzan

He is Tarzan

He is Tarzan and he lives in the jungle.

Peachie Speechie's
R Sound Chaining

AR

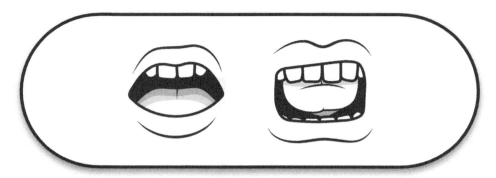

Ar
⇩
Far
⇩
Afar
⇩
Came from afar
⇩
They came from afar to see the ball game.

PEACHIE SPEECHIE'S
R SOUND CHAINING

AR

Ar

⇩

Star

⇩

Starry

⇩

Starry night

⇩

It was a clear starry night.

PEACHIE SPEECHIE'S
R SOUND CHAINING

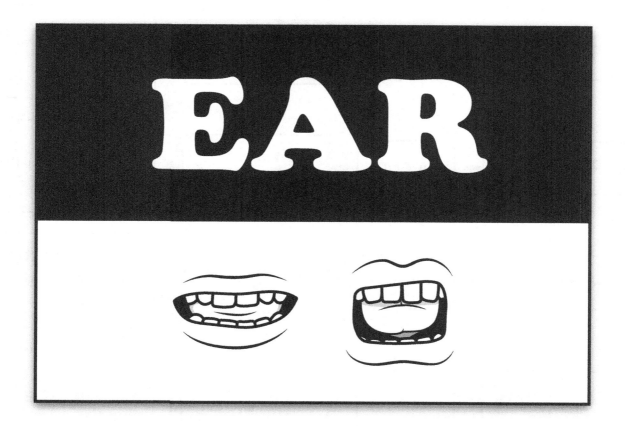

R SOUND CHAINING
by Peachie Speechie

Directions: Start by saying the first utterance in the chain several times. Then, move to the next utterance in the chain. They become longer and more complex as you go.

BONUS: Can you make up your own sentences using the bolded phrases below?

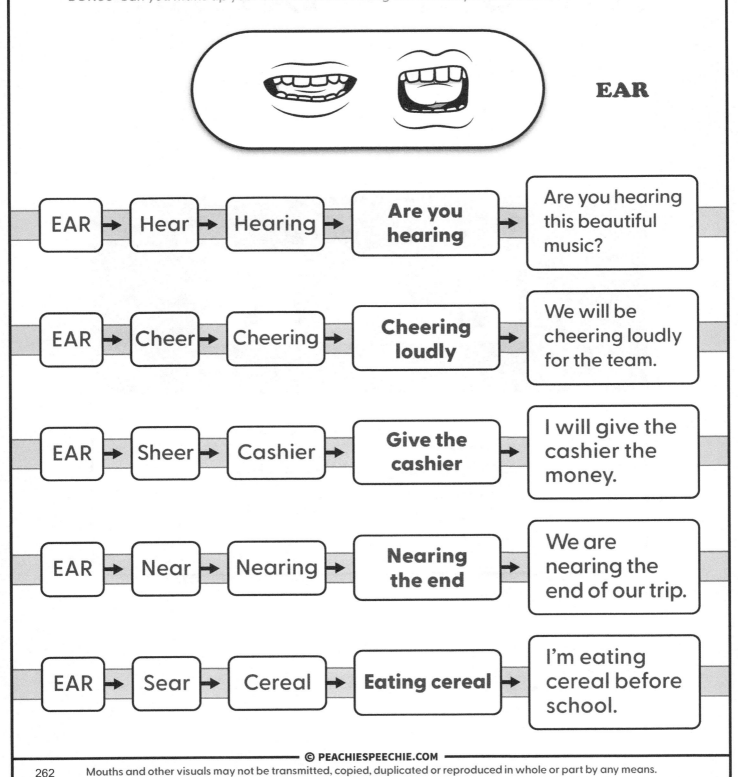

EAR → Hear → Hearing → **Are you hearing** → Are you hearing this beautiful music?

EAR → Cheer → Cheering → **Cheering loudly** → We will be cheering loudly for the team.

EAR → Sheer → Cashier → **Give the cashier** → I will give the cashier the money.

EAR → Near → Nearing → **Nearing the end** → We are nearing the end of our trip.

EAR → Sear → Cereal → **Eating cereal** → I'm eating cereal before school.

Peachie Speechie's
R Sound Chaining

EAR

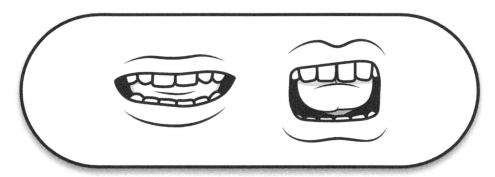

Ear
⇩
Cheer
⇩
Cheering
⇩
Cheering crowd
⇩
Did you hear the cheering crowd?

PEACHIE SPEECHIE'S
R SOUND CHAINING

EAR

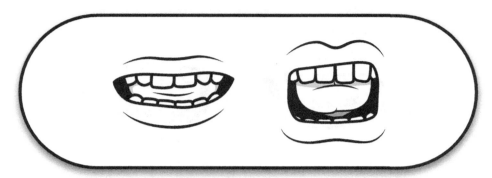

Ear
⇩
Peer
⇩
Appeared
⇩
It just appeared
⇩
It just appeared out of nowhere!

Peachie Speechie's
R Sound Chaining

EAR

Ear
⇩
Steer
⇩
Steering
⇩
Steering wheel
⇩
Turn the steering wheel to the left.

PEACHIE SPEECHIE'S
R SOUND CHAINING

EAR

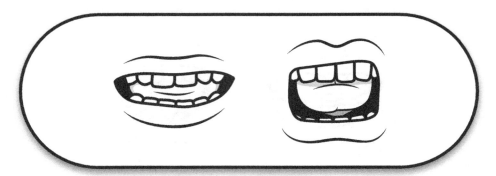

Ear
⇩
Beard
⇩
Bearded
⇩
The bearded dragon
⇩
The bearded dragon was my favorite thing at the zoo.

R SOUND CHAINING

EAR

Ear
⇩
Fear
⇩
Fearful
⇩
She's fearful
⇩
She's fearful of the ocean.

PEACHIE SPEECHIE'S
R SOUND CHAINING

EAR

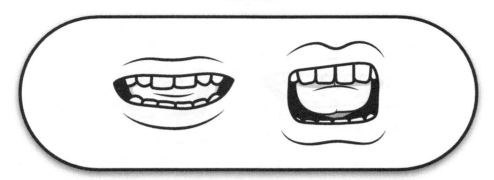

Ear
⇩
Hear
⇩
Hearing
⇩
Hearing aid
⇩
My pappa wears a hearing aid.

PEACHIE SPEECHIE'S
R SOUND CHAINING

EAR

Ear
⇩
Tear
⇩
Cafeteria
⇩
In the cafeteria
⇩
Let's go eat in the cafeteria.

PEACHIE SPEECHIE'S
R SOUND CHAINING

EAR

Ear
⇩
Peer
⇩
Period
⇩
Period of time
⇩
We waited for a long period of time.

Peachie Speechie's
R Sound Chaining

EAR

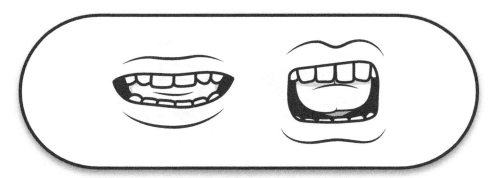

Ear

⇩

Peer

⇩

Pyramids

⇩

Ancient pyramids

⇩

We learned about the ancient pyramids at school.

Peachie Speechie's R Sound Chaining

EAR

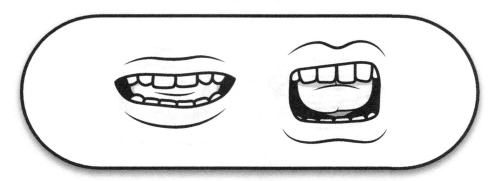

Ear

⇩

Sear

⇩

Cereal

⇩

Eating cereal

⇩

I am eating cereal for breakfast again.

Peachie Speechie's R Sound Chaining

EAR

Ear
⇩
Sheer
⇩
Cashier
⇩
The helpful cashier
⇩
The helpful cashier put my items in a bag.

Peachie Speechie's
R Sound Chaining

EAR

Ear
⇩
Clear
⇩
Unclear
⇩
Was unclear
⇩
The purpose of the event was unclear.

Peachie Speechie's R Sound Chaining

EAR

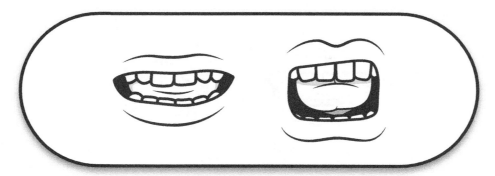

Ear
⇩
Pier
⇩
Piercing
⇩
Piercing my nose
⇩
I'm thinking about piercing my nose.

Peachie Speechie's
R Sound Chaining

EAR

Ear
⇩
Peer
⇩
Disappeared
⇩
Just disappeared
⇩
The balloons just disappeared into the sky.

PEACHIE SPEECHIE'S
R SOUND CHAINING

EAR

Ear
⇩
Hear
⇩
Hero
⇩
Super hero
⇩
The super hero flew across the sky.

PEACHIE SPEECHIE'S
R SOUND CHAINING

EAR

Ear
⇩
Spear
⇩
Spirit
⇩
School spirit
⇩
I'm showing my school spirit today.

Peachie Speechie's R Sound Chaining

EAR

Ear
⇩
Clear
⇩
Clearing
⇩
In the clearing
⇩
We had a picnic in the clearing by the woods.

PEACHIE SPEECHIE'S
R SOUND CHAINING

EAR

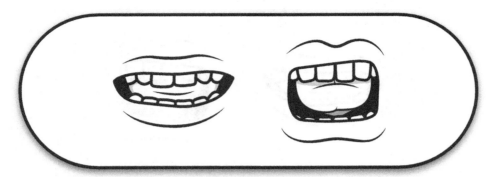

Ear
⇩
Smear
⇩
Smearing
⇩
Smearing cream cheese
⇩
I'm smearing cream cheese on my bagel.

PEACHIE SPEECHIE'S
R SOUND CHAINING

EAR

Ear
⇩
Near
⇩
Nearing
⇩
Is nearing
⇩
The plane is nearing its destination.

PEACHIE SPEECHIE'S
R SOUND CHAINING

EAR

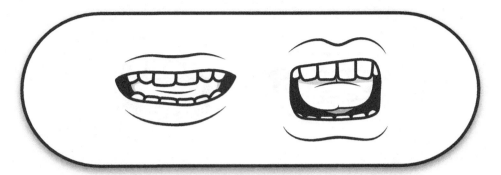

Ear
⇩
Gear
⇩
Gearing
⇩
Gearing up
⇩
We are gearing up for the holiday season.

PEACHIE SPEECHIE'S
R SOUND CHAINING

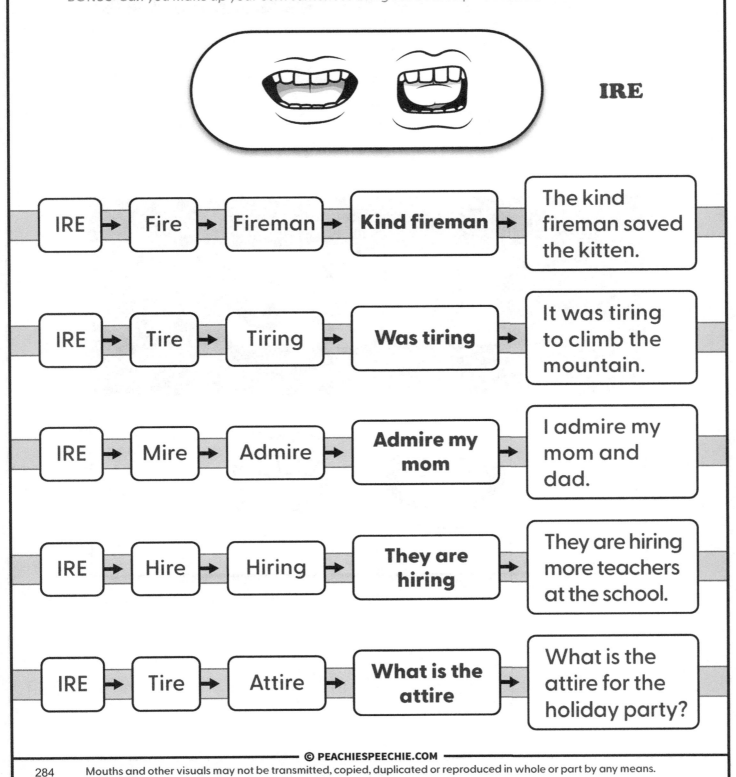

PEACHIE SPEECHIE'S
R SOUND CHAINING

IRE

Ire
⇩
Wire
⇩
Wiring
⇩
Fix the wiring
⇩
We had to fix the wiring in the robot.

PEACHIE SPEECHIE'S
R SOUND CHAINING

IRE

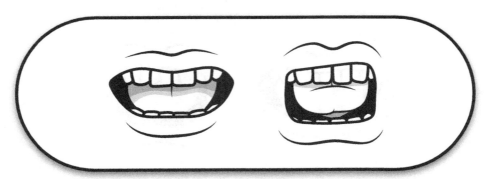

Ire
⇩
Tire
⇩
Tiring
⇩
Tiring day
⇩
It was a long and tiring day.

PEACHIE SPEECHIE'S
R SOUND CHAINING

IRE

Ire
⇩
Hire
⇩
Hiring
⇩
Hiring a cook
⇩
My favorite restaurant is hiring a cook.

PEACHIE SPEECHIE'S
R SOUND CHAINING

IRE

Ire

⇩

Pire

⇩

Umpire

⇩

The umpire called

⇩

The umpire called him out of the game.

Peachie Speechie's R SOUND CHAINING

IRE

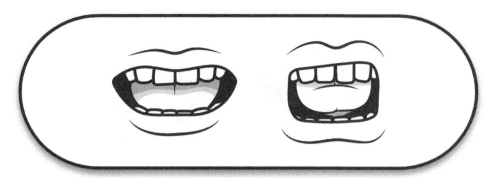

Ire
⇩
Quire
⇩
Inquired
⇩
Inquired about
⇩
I called and inquired about the job.

Peachie Speechie's R Sound Chaining

IRE

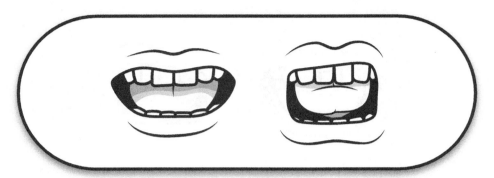

Ire
⇩
Mire
⇩
Admired
⇩
Admired her
⇩
I admired her work in the museum.

Peachie Speechie's
R Sound Chaining

IRE

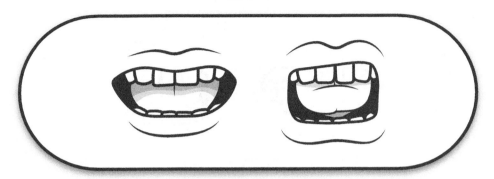

Ire
⇩
Fire
⇩
Fiery
⇩
The fiery pit
⇩
She tossed it into the fiery pit.

PEACHIE SPEECHIE'S
R SOUND CHAINING

IRE

Ire
⇩
Quire
⇩
Requirement
⇩
What's the requirement
⇩
What's the requirement for this project?

PEACHIE SPEECHIE'S
R SOUND CHAINING

IRE

Ire

⇩

Fire

⇩

Firewood

⇩

Collect firewood

⇩

We collect firewood when we go camping.

PEACHIE SPEECHIE'S
R SOUND CHAINING

IRE

Ire

⇩

Quire

⇩

Acquired

⇩

Acquired it

⇩

I acquired it at the yard sale.

PEACHIE SPEECHIE'S
R SOUND CHAINING

IRE

Ire
⇩
Zire
⇩
Desire
⇩
Do you desire
⇩
What do you desire most?

PEACHIE SPEECHIE'S
R SOUND CHAINING

IRE

Ire
⇩
Fire
⇩
Sapphire
⇩
Blue sapphire
⇩
The blue sapphire ring is special.

R SOUND CHAINING

IRE

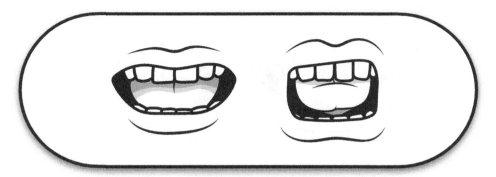

Ire
⇩
Tire
⇩
Attire
⇩
Fanciest attire
⇩
Wear your fanciest attire to the wedding.

PEACHIE SPEECHIE'S
R SOUND CHAINING

IRE

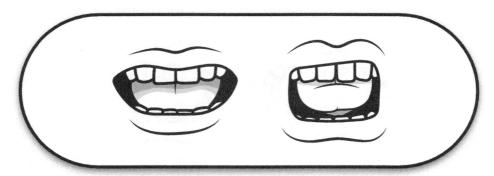

Ire
⇩
Spire
⇩
Aspire
⇩
Aspire to be
⇩
I aspire to be a musician.

PEACHIE SPEECHIE'S
R SOUND CHAINING

R SOUND CHAINING
by Peachie Speechie

Directions: Start by saying the first utterance in the chain several times. Then, move to the next utterance in the chain. They become longer and more complex as you go.

BONUS: Can you make up your own sentences using the bolded phrases below?

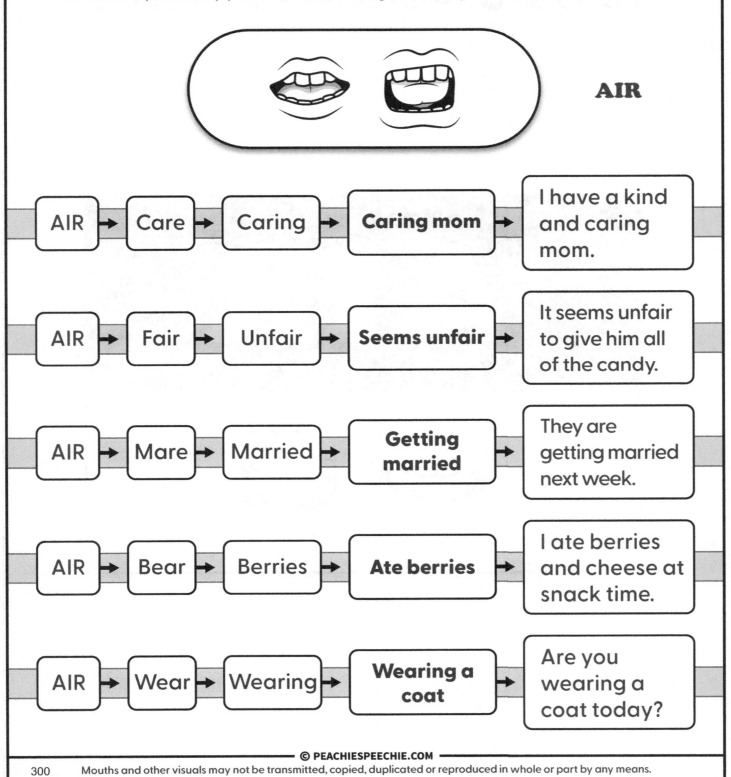

AIR

AIR → Care → Caring → **Caring mom** → I have a kind and caring mom.

AIR → Fair → Unfair → **Seems unfair** → It seems unfair to give him all of the candy.

AIR → Mare → Married → **Getting married** → They are getting married next week.

AIR → Bear → Berries → **Ate berries** → I ate berries and cheese at snack time.

AIR → Wear → Wearing → **Wearing a coat** → Are you wearing a coat today?

Peachie Speechie's
R Sound Chaining

AIR

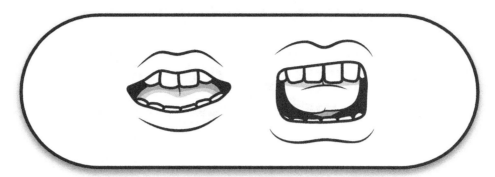

Air
⇩
Tare
⇩
Terrible
⇩
Feel terrible
⇩
I feel terrible after eating all the candy.

PEACHIE SPEECHIE'S
R SOUND CHAINING

AIR

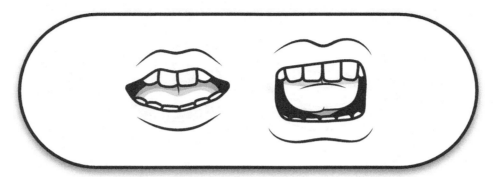

Air
⇩
Care
⇩
Carried
⇩
Carried the bag
⇩
He carried the bag for me.

Peachie Speechie's R Sound Chaining

AIR

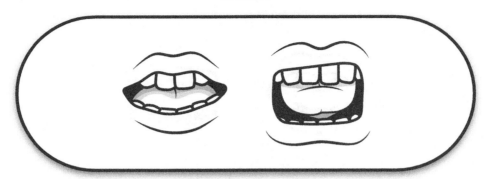

Air
⇩
Dare
⇩
Daring
⇩
Daring decision
⇩
He made a daring decision.

PEACHIE SPEECHIE'S
R SOUND CHAINING

AIR

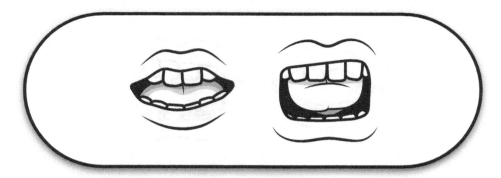

Air
⇩
Hair
⇩
Hairy
⇩
Hairy dog
⇩
I've never seen such a hairy dog!

PEACHIE SPEECHIE'S
R SOUND CHAINING

AIR

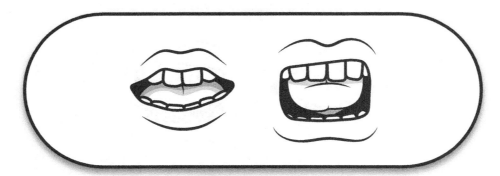

Air
⇩
Care
⇩
Caring
⇩
Kind and caring
⇩
She is a kind and caring person.

PEACHIE SPEECHIE'S
R SOUND CHAINING

AIR

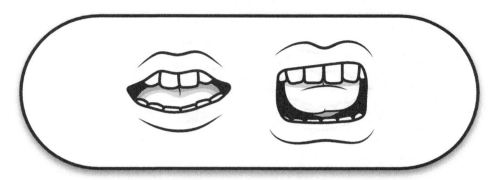

Air

⇩

Wear

⇩

Wearing

⇩

Wearing it around

⇩

I've been wearing it around the house.

Peachie Speechie's R Sound Chaining

AIR

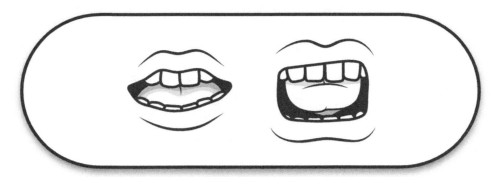

Air
⇩
Scare
⇩
Scaring
⇩
Scaring the cat
⇩
The barking dog is scaring the cat.

PEACHIE SPEECHIE'S
R SOUND CHAINING

AIR

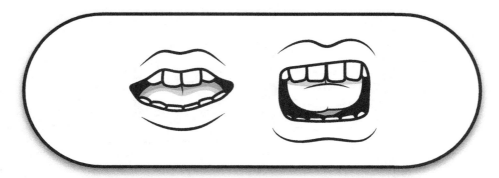

Air

Pears

Repairs

Needs repairs

The car needs repairs before you can drive it.

Peachie Speechie's R Sound Chaining

AIR

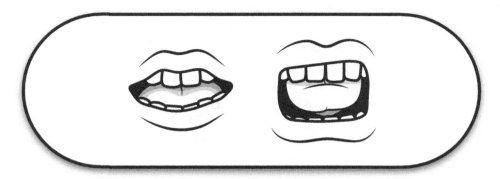

Air
⇩
Care
⇩
Carefully
⇩
Carefully holding
⇩
She is carefully holding the baby.

Peachie Speechie's
R Sound Chaining

AIR

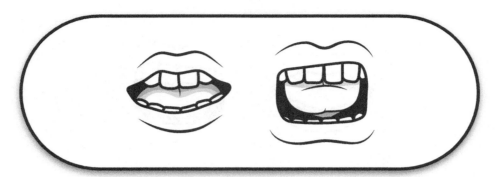

Air

⇩

Wear

⇩

Aware

⇩

Are you aware?

⇩

Are you aware of what happened last night?

PEACHIE SPEECHIE'S
R SOUND CHAINING

AIR

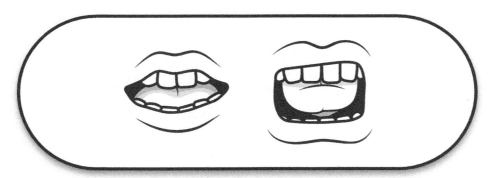

Air

Pare

Parents

My loving parents

My loving parents sent me a birthday card.

PEACHIE SPEECHIE'S
R SOUND CHAINING

AIR

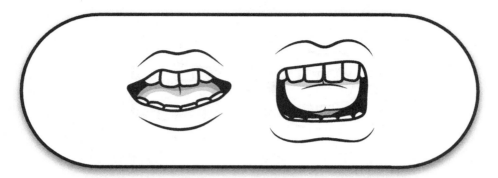

Air

Bear

Buried
⇩
Buried the bone

The dog buried the bone outside.

PEACHIE SPEECHIE'S
R SOUND CHAINING

AIR

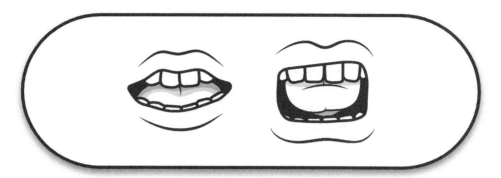

Air

Bear

Barrel

Barrel of candy

There was a barrel of candy at the market.

PEACHIE SPEECHIE'S
R SOUND CHAINING

AIR

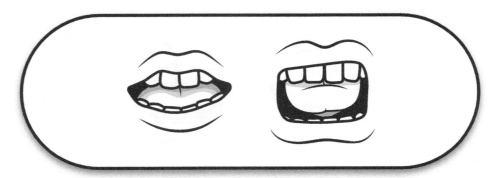

Air
⇩
Bear
⇩
Berries
⇩
Fresh berries
⇩
I put fresh berries in the pie.

PEACHIE SPEECHIE'S
R SOUND CHAINING

AIR

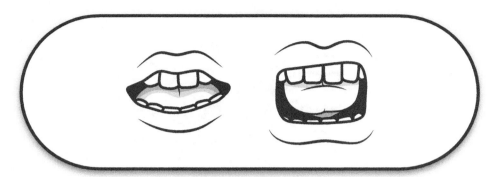

Air
⇩
Chair
⇩
Chairman
⇩
He's the chairman
⇩
He's the chairman of the organization.

PEACHIE SPEECHIE'S
R SOUND CHAINING

AIR

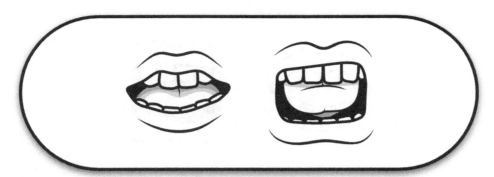

Air
⇩
Stare
⇩
Staring
⇩
You staring
⇩
Hey, what are you staring at?

Peachie Speechie's R Sound Chaining

AIR

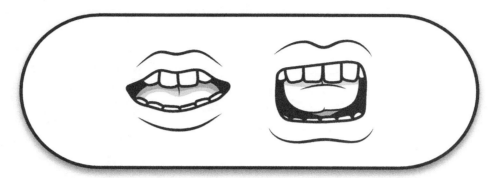

Air
⇩
Mare
⇩
Marigolds
⇩
Bouquet of marigolds
⇩
He brought me a bouquet of marigolds.

PEACHIE SPEECHIE'S
R SOUND CHAINING

AIR

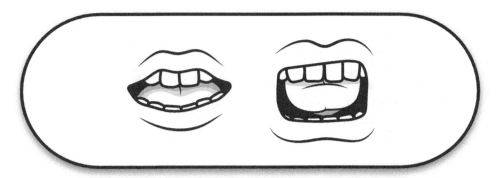

Air
⇩
Mare
⇩
Marilyn
⇩
Named Marilyn
⇩
My niece is named Marilyn.

Peachie Speechie's R SOUND CHAINING

AIR

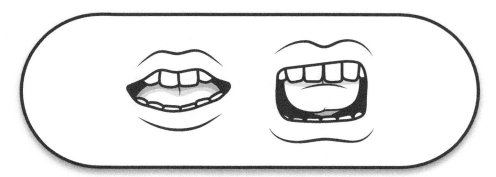

Air
⇩
Pair
⇩
Paradise
⇩
Tropical paradise
⇩
We vacationed to a tropical paradise.

PEACHIE SPEECHIE'S
R SOUND CHAINING

AIR

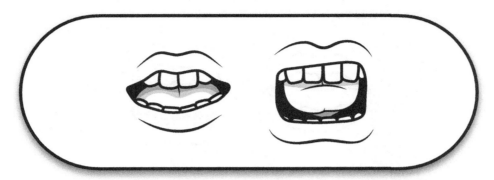

Air

Pare

Parrot

Talking parrot

Have you seen the talking parrot?

PEACHIE SPEECHIE'S
R SOUND CHAINING

AIR

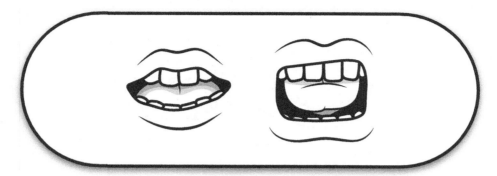

Air
⇩
Pare
⇩
Parakeet
⇩
Pet parakeet
⇩
I would like a pet parakeet.

Peachie Speechie's
R Sound Chaining

AIR

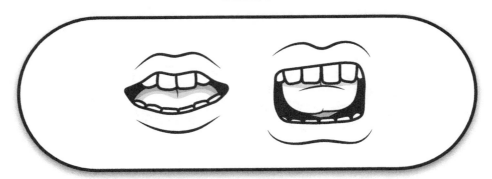

Air

⇩

Tear

⇩

Terrified

⇩

Was terrified

⇩

She saw a snake and was terrified.

Peachie Speechie's
R Sound Chaining

AIR

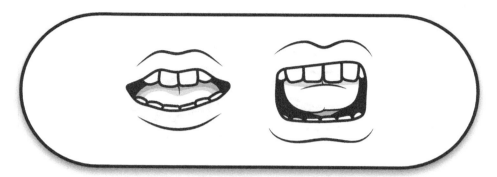

Air
⇩
Tear
⇩
Tearing
⇩
Tearing it
⇩
The dog is tearing it with his teeth.

PEACHIE SPEECHIE'S
R SOUND CHAINING

AIR

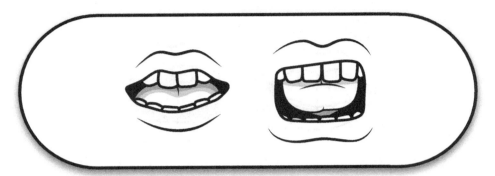

Air
⇩
Share
⇩
Sharon
⇩
Aunt Sharon
⇩
Is Aunt Sharon coming to dinner?

PEACHIE SPEECHIE'S
R SOUND CHAINING

AIR

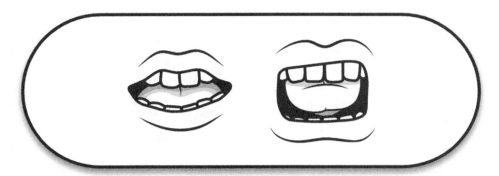

Air
⇩
Claire
⇩
Clarinet
⇩
Play the clarinet
⇩
I want to play the clarinet.

PEACHIE SPEECHIE'S
R SOUND CHAINING

AIR

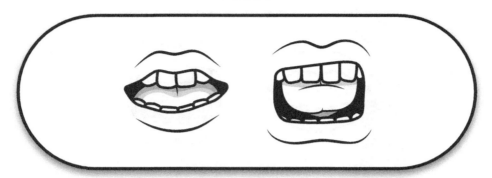

Air

⇩

Care

⇩

Carriage

⇩

Pull the carriage

⇩

The big horse will pull the carriage.

Peachie Speechie's R Sound Chaining

AIR

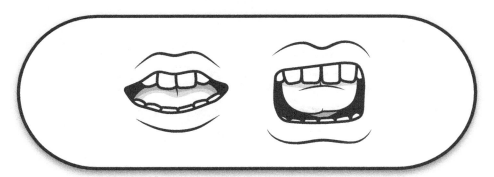

Air
⇩
Dare
⇩
Dairy
⇩
Dairy cow
⇩
Bessie is our family's dairy cow.

PEACHIE SPEECHIE'S
R SOUND CHAINING

AIR

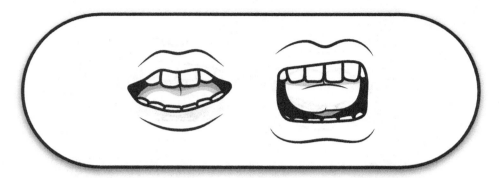

Air
⇩
Mare
⇩
Married
⇩
Getting married
⇩
The happy couple is getting married.

PEACHIE SPEECHIE'S
R SOUND CHAINING

AIR

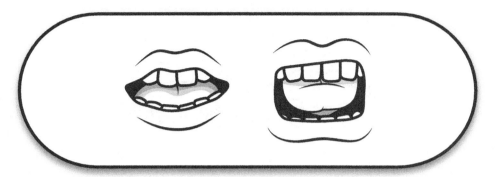

Air
⇩
Nare
⇩
Narrow
⇩
Narrow path
⇩
We walked down the narrow path.

Mouths and other visuals may not be transmitted, copied, duplicated or reproduced in whole or part by any means.

PEACHIE SPEECHIE'S
R SOUND CHAINING

AIR

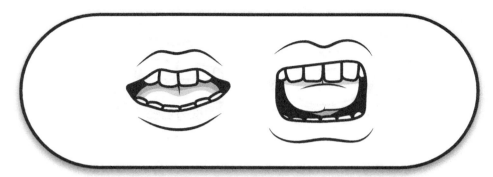

Air

Tear

Terrace

On the terrace

We had tea out on the terrace.

PEACHIE SPEECHIE'S
R SOUND CHAINING

AIR

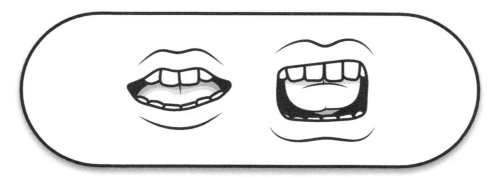

Air
⇩
Chair
⇩
Cherry
⇩
Cherry pie
⇩
I want to make a cherry pie.

PEACHIE SPEECHIE'S
R SOUND CHAINING

AIR

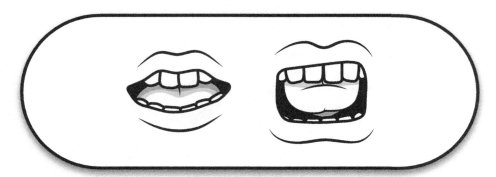

Air
⇩
Fair
⇩
Fairy
⇩
Fairy dust
⇩
Sprinkle some magic fairy dust on it.

PEACHIE SPEECHIE'S
R SOUND CHAINING

AIR

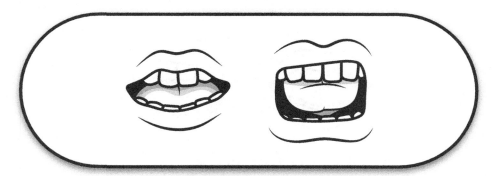

Air
⇩
Share
⇩
Cheryl
⇩
Miss Cheryl
⇩
Miss Cheryl is our music teacher.

PEACHIE SPEECHIE'S
R SOUND CHAINING

AIR

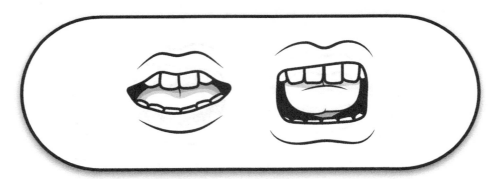

Air
⇩
Mare
⇩
Merry
⇩
Merry Christmas
⇩
We wish you a merry Christmas.

Peachie Speechie's
R Sound Chaining

AIR

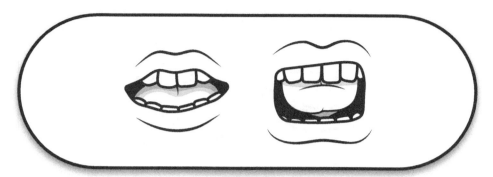

Air
⇩
Pair
⇩
Paris
⇩
Visit Paris
⇩
I would like to visit Paris one day.

PEACHIE SPEECHIE'S
R SOUND CHAINING

AIR

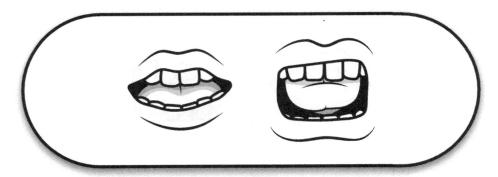

Air

⇩

Pare

⇩

Sparrow

⇩

Sparrow singing

⇩

Do you hear the sparrow singing in the tree?

PEACHIE SPEECHIE'S
R SOUND CHAINING

AIR

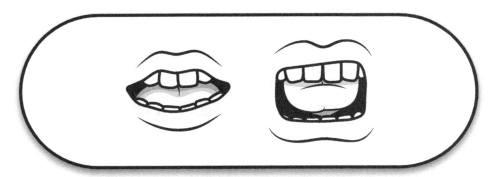

Air

⇩

Fair

⇩

Fahrenheit

⇩

Degrees Fahrenheit

⇩

It is 32 degrees Fahrenheit outside.

PEACHIE SPEECHIE'S
R SOUND CHAINING

AIR

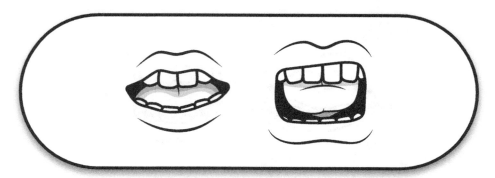

Air
⇩
Hair
⇩
Heritage
⇩
My heritage
⇩
I'm learning about my heritage.

Peachie Speechie's
R Sound Chaining

AIR

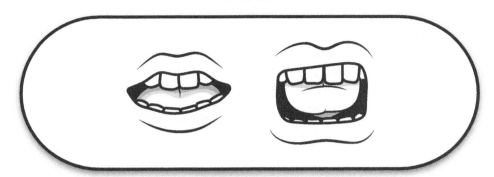

Air
⇩
Mare
⇩
Maryland
⇩
State of Maryland
⇩
I'm moving to the state of Maryland.

PEACHIE SPEECHIE'S
R SOUND CHAINING

AIR

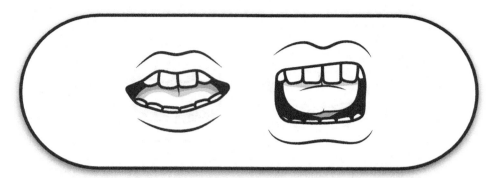

Air
⇩
Pare
⇩
Parachute
⇩
Need a parachute
⇩
You'll need a parachute to go skydiving.

PEACHIE SPEECHIE'S
R SOUND CHAINING

AIR

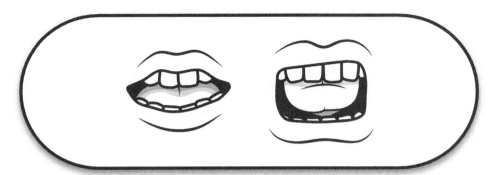

Air
⇩
Pare
⇩
Parallel
⇩
Parallel lines
⇩
Draw two parallel lines.

Peachie Speechie's
R Sound Chaining

AIR

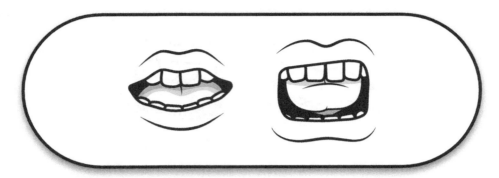

Air

Care

Carrot

Eat the carrot

Will you eat the carrot?

PEACHIE SPEECHIE'S
R SOUND CHAINING

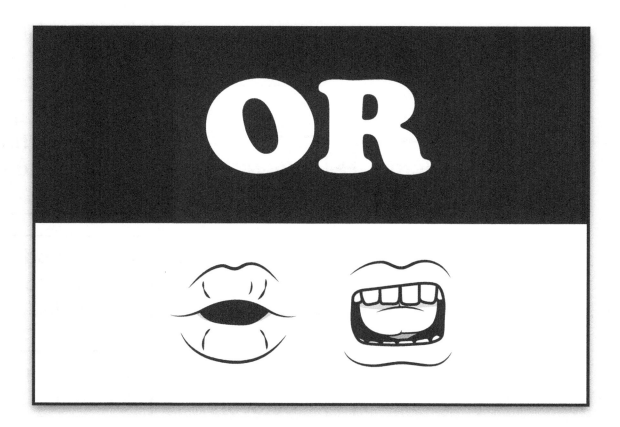

R SOUND CHAINING
by Peachie Speechie

Directions: Start by saying the first utterance in the chain several times. Then, move to the next utterance in the chain. They become longer and more complex as you go.

BONUS: Can you make up your own sentences using the bolded phrases below?

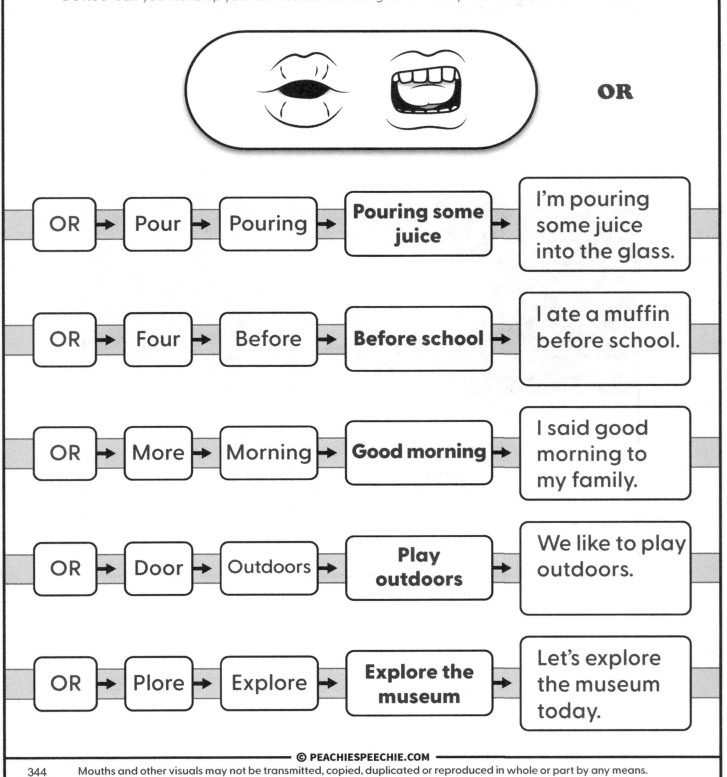

OR → Pour → Pouring → **Pouring some juice** → I'm pouring some juice into the glass.

OR → Four → Before → **Before school** → I ate a muffin before school.

OR → More → Morning → **Good morning** → I said good morning to my family.

OR → Door → Outdoors → **Play outdoors** → We like to play outdoors.

OR → Plore → Explore → **Explore the museum** → Let's explore the museum today.

PEACHIE SPEECHIE'S
R SOUND CHAINING

Or

Or
⇩
Form
⇩
Formula
⇩
Secret formula
⇩
Do you know the secret formula?

PEACHIE SPEECHIE'S
R SOUND CHAINING

OR

Or
⇩
Corn
⇩
Popcorn
⇩
Eating popcorn
⇩
We are eating popcorn in the theater.

Peachie Speechie's
R Sound Chaining

OR

Or
⇩
Torn
⇩
Tornado
⇩
Tornado was spinning
⇩
The tornado was spinning and knocking down trees.

PEACHIE SPEECHIE'S
R SOUND CHAINING

OR

Or
⇩
Store
⇩
Storage
⇩
Storage closet
⇩
Put the supplies in the storage closet.

PEACHIE SPEECHIE'S
R SOUND CHAINING

OR

Or
⇩
For
⇩
Forest
⇩
Dark spooky forest
⇩
I don't want to go into the dark, spooky forest.

PEACHIE SPEECHIE'S
R SOUND CHAINING

OR

Or
⇩
More
⇩
Morning
⇩
Sunday morning
⇩
I woke up early Sunday morning.

Peachie Speechie's
R Sound Chaining

OR

Or
⇩
Bore
⇩
Boring
⇩
Boring lesson
⇩
I have to sit through a boring lesson.

Peachie Speechie's
R SOUND CHAINING

OR

Or

⇩

Store

⇩

Story

⇩

Story time

⇩

The library is hosting story time today.

PEACHIE SPEECHIE'S
R SOUND CHAINING

OR

Or
⇩
Door
⇩
Dorothy
⇩
Know Dorothy
⇩
Do you know Dorothy?

PEACHIE SPEECHIE'S
R SOUND CHAINING

OR

Or
⇩
Floor
⇩
Florida
⇩
Been to Florida
⇩
Have you been to Florida?

PEACHIE SPEECHIE'S
R SOUND CHAINING

OR

Or
⇩
Core
⇩
Decor
⇩
Love the decor
⇩
I love the decor in your home.

PEACHIE SPEECHIE'S
R SOUND CHAINING

OR

Or
⇩
Core
⇩
Coral
⇩
See the coral
⇩
Did you see the coral in the ocean?

PEACHIE SPEECHIE'S
R SOUND CHAINING

OR

Or
⇩
Door
⇩
Doreen
⇩
Aunt Doreen
⇩
Aunt Doreen is coming to visit.

PEACHIE SPEECHIE'S
R SOUND CHAINING

OR

Or
⇩
Floor
⇩
Flooring
⇩
New flooring
⇩
They put new flooring in the classroom.

PEACHIE SPEECHIE'S
R SOUND CHAINING

OR

Or
⇩
For
⇩
Foreign
⇩
Foreign country
⇩
I want to travel to a foreign country.

PEACHIE SPEECHIE'S
R SOUND CHAINING

OR

Or
⇩
Lore
⇩
Loren
⇩
Name is Loren
⇩
Hello, my name is Loren.

Peachie Speechie's
R Sound Chaining

OR

Or

Core

Courses

Taking courses
⇩
Are you taking courses at the community college?

Peachie Speechie's
R Sound Chaining

OR

Or
⇩
Pour
⇩
Pouring
⇩
Pouring milk
⇩
I'm pouring milk in a glass.

PEACHIE SPEECHIE'S
R SOUND CHAINING

OR

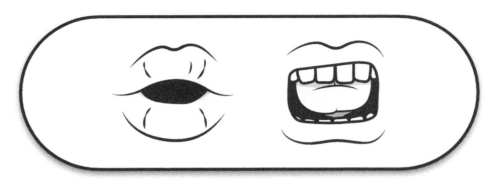

Or
⇩
Four
⇩
Forty
⇩
Forty-seven cents
⇩
The candy costs forty-seven cents.

PEACHIE SPEECHIE'S
R SOUND CHAINING

OR

Or
⇩
Nor
⇩
Ignore
⇩
Impossible to ignore
⇩
It was impossible to ignore my dog's cute face.

Peachie Speechie's
R Sound Chaining

Or

Or
⇩
Door
⇩
Outdoors
⇩
Worked outdoors
⇩
We worked outdoors all day long.

PEACHIE SPEECHIE'S
R SOUND CHAINING

OR

Or
⇩
Door
⇩
Adore
⇩
Adore you
⇩
I absolutely adore you.

PEACHIE SPEECHIE'S
R SOUND CHAINING

OR

Or
⇩
Plore
⇩
Exploring
⇩
I'm exploring
⇩
I'm exploring the campsite today.

PEACHIE SPEECHIE'S
R SOUND CHAINING

OR

Or

Corn

Acorn

Found an acorn

⇩

The little chipmunk found an acorn.

PEACHIE SPEECHIE'S
R SOUND CHAINING

L→R Slide & Chaining

Many speech-language pathologists elicit an R sound by shaping it from the L sound. This is done by having clients start with the tongue in position for /l/ and then sliding their tongue back along the roof of the mouth to achieve placement for a retroflex /ɹ/. The following pages combine shaping and chaining. Each chain simply starts with the L→R slide, which sounds like "ler".

While these follow a slightly different pattern from the other chains in the book, SLPs might find them helpful in practicing the R sound with students.

You may want to practice the L→R slide in isolation prior to moving on to the chains. Use the visuals below as you practice.

L→R Slide

Start by placing your tongue tip on your alveolar ridge for the /l/ sound. Turn your voice on and sustain /l/.

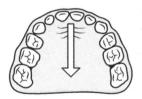
Next, keep your voice on and slide your tongue tip back along the roof of your mouth.

Your tongue will form a bowl shape for retroflex R and you'll hear the sound change.

Peachie Speechie's R Sound Chaining

L→R

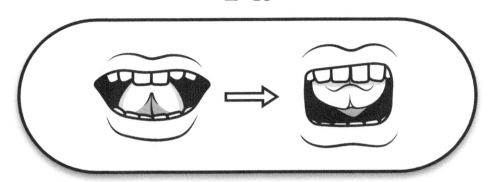

L→R
⇩
Learn
⇩
Learning
⇩
Always learning
⇩
I am always learning new things.

PEACHIE SPEECHIE'S
R SOUND CHAINING

L→R

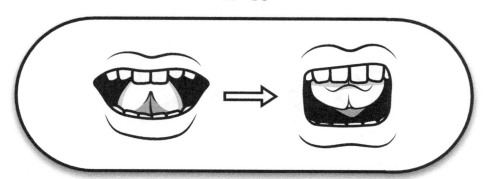

L→R

⇩

Lurk

⇩

Lurking

⇩

Was lurking in

⇩

The goblin was lurking in the shadows.

PEACHIE SPEECHIE'S
R SOUND CHAINING

L→R

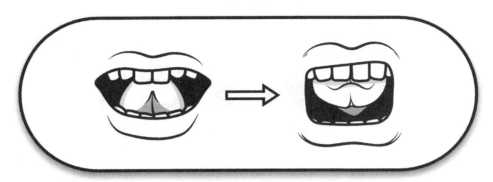

L→R
⇩
Oller
⇩
Collar
⇩
Dog collar
⇩
The dog collar is in the closet.

PEACHIE SPEECHIE'S
R SOUND CHAINING

L→R

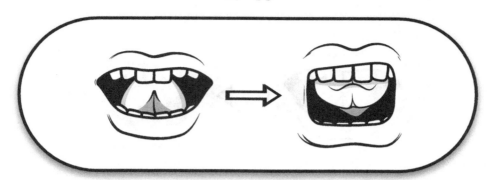

L→R
⇩
Aller
⇩
Smaller
⇩
He is smaller
⇩
He is smaller than I am.

PEACHIE SPEECHIE'S
R SOUND CHAINING

L→R

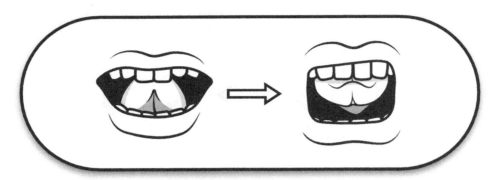

L→R
⇩
Lers
⇩
Dollars
⇩
Many dollars
⇩
How many dollars do you need?

PEACHIE SPEECHIE'S
R SOUND CHAINING

L→R

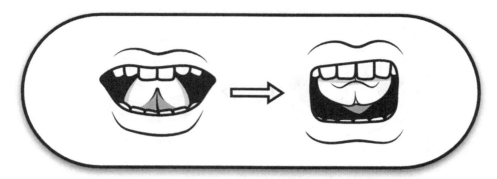

L→R

⇩

Lers

⇩

Colors

⇩

Five colors

⇩

She painted five colors on the wall.

PEACHIE SPEECHIE'S
R SOUND CHAINING

Make your own R sound chain.

⬛ SYLLABLE
⇩
⬛ SINGLE SYLLABLE WORD
⇩
⬛ MULTISYLLABIC WORD
⇩
⬛ PHRASE
⇩
⬛ SENTENCE

Resources

Johnson, H.P., & Hood, S.B. (1988). Teaching chaining to unintelligible children: How to deal with open syllables. *Language, Speech, and Hearing Services in the School (19)2*, 211-220.

Kaufman, N. (n.d.) The successive approximation method of speech therapy for children with childhood apraxia of speech. *Apraxia Kids*. https://www.apraxia-kids.org/apraxia_kids_library/the-successive-approximation-method-of-therapy-for-children-with-apraxia-of-speech/

Preston, J., Leece M., & Storto, J. (2019). Tutorial: Speech motor chaining treatment for school-aged children with speech sound disorders. *Language, Speech and Hearing Services in Schools, 50,* 343-355.

Lindsay, L. (2020). *Speaking of apraxia: Parents' guide to childhood apraxia of speech*. 2nd. ed. Woodbine House.

PEACHIE SPEECHIE'S
R SOUND CHAINING

About the Author

Meredith Avren is an ASHA certified speech-language pathologist, public speaker, and author of many popular speech therapy workbooks. She is known for her "I Can Say…" workbook series focusing on remediation of speech sound disorders. She has over 10 years of experience in the school-based setting, and considers the R sound to be her specialty. Meredith graduated from Georgia State University, and lives in the Atlanta area with her graphic designer husband, Josh, and their sons.

Contact Meredith: meredith@peachiespeechie.com

Made in the USA
Middletown, DE
30 October 2023

41502087R00212